T0316576

Bad News from Venezuela

Since the election of President Hugo Chavez in 1998, Venezuela has become an important news item. Western coverage is shaped by the cultural milieu of its journalists, with news written from New York or London by non-specialists or by those staying inside wealthy guarded enclaves in an intensely segregated Caracas. Journalists mainly work with English-speaking elites and have little contact with the poor majority. Therefore, they reproduce ideas largely attuned to a Western, neoliberal understanding of Venezuela.

Through extensive analysis of media coverage from Chavez's election to the present day, as well as detailed interviews with journalists and academics covering the country, *Bad News from Venezuela* highlights the factors contributing to reportage in Venezuela and why those factors exist in the first place. From this examination of a single Latin American country, the book furthers the discussion of contemporary media in the West, and how, with the rise of 'fake news', their operations have a significant impact on the wider representation of global affairs.

Bad News from Venezuela is comprehensive and enlightening for undergraduate students and research academics in media and Latin American studies.

Alan MacLeod is a member of the Glasgow Media Group and completed his thesis in sociology in 2017. He specialized in media theory and analysis.

Routledge Focus on Communication and Society
Series Editor: James Curran

Routledge Focus on Communication and Society offers both established and early-career academics the flexibility to publish cutting-edge analysis on topical issues, research on new media or in-depth case studies within the broad field of media, communication and cultural studies. Its main concerns are whether the media empower or fail to empower popular forces in society; media organisations and public policy; and the political and social consequences of the media.

Bad News from Venezuela
Alan MacLeod

For a complete list of titles in this series, please see: www.routledge.com/series/SE0130

Bad News from Venezuela

Twenty years of fake news
and misreporting

Alan MacLeod

Routledge
Taylor & Francis Group

LONDON AND NEW YORK

First published 2018 by Routledge

2 Park Square, Milton Park, Abingdon, Oxon OX14 4RN
605 Third Avenue, New York, NY 10017

*Routledge is an imprint of the Taylor & Francis Group, an
informa business*

First issued in paperback 2021

Publisher's Note

The publisher has gone to great lengths to ensure the quality of this reprint
but points out that some imperfections in the original copies may be apparent.

British Library Cataloguing-in-Publication Data
A catalogue record for this book is available from the British
Library

Library of Congress Cataloging-in-Publication Data
A catalog record for this book has been requested

ISBN: 978-1-138-48923-3 (hbk)
ISBN: 978-1-03-217875-2 (pbk)
DOI: 10.4324/9781351038263

Typeset in Sabon
by Apex CoVantage, LLC

To my parents

Contents

Tables

Introduction

The idea of "fake news" was popularized by Hillary Clinton's campaign and much of the mainstream media, who claimed it was a key factor in the election of Donald Trump as President. However, it immediately rebounded upon them as Trump began to use it against them. It, and its close synonym "post truth", have become key terms of our era, with the latter awarded 2016's word of the year by Oxford Dictionaries. Fake news has come to be understood as false or deceptive, excessively biased, low-quality journalism. It did not start with Trump, however. Indeed, Herman and Chomsky (1988) have shown that the media has continually pushed false narratives in order to brainwash the population into agreeing with whatever elites wish for decades.

The coverage of Venezuela fits into this perfectly. In 2002, in the midst of a violent coup against him, the media claimed President Hugo Chavez had resigned after ordering a massacre (see Chapter 2) while in 2014 they presented a violent radical uprising aimed at overthrowing the government through terror as a peaceful protest against crime, hunger and government oppression (see Chapter 5).

Why the media would have a stake in presenting Venezuela in such a way is a seriously interesting question. There are few other places that would elect a former hippie turned bus driver turned politician as President like Venezuela did with Nicolas Maduro in 2013. The worldwide interest in Venezuela is a relatively new phenomenon and can be directly traced back to the 1998 election of Chavez. Suddenly the country had a President who would call President George Bush a "donkey" and a "devil".

Chavez was a highly controversial figure in the West, with the conservative Heritage Foundation claiming Venezuela had become a "terrorist state" (Walser, 2010) while others on the left presenting him and the country to be a shining inspiration for all those who believe a better world is possible.

Chavez's outbursts are well-known. What is less known is the radical change occurring in Venezuelan society. Millions of ordinary Venezuelans claim to have been empowered by the Chavez government (1998–2013), who used the profits from the oil industry to drastically reduce poverty, inequality, illiteracy and hunger and fostered a sense of inclusion, changing the constitution and creating a new, truly participatory, popular democratic model. Critics, on the other hand, have seen his and his successor, Nicolas Maduro's moves as destroying a once great democratic nation by removing checks and balances on popular will, effectively turning the country into a dictatorship.

Chavez pioneered the ideology of 21st century socialism, which directly challenges both American dominance of Latin America and the ideology of neoliberalism, with its emphasis on the free-market, private ownership, competition, globalization and minimal government regulation or interference in the economy. His example helped inspire a wave of leftist governments to come to power across Latin America, like in Brazil, Bolivia and Ecuador, who have challenged the elites in their own countries as well as the United States. It has also inspired a new wave of anti-neoliberal left parties across Europe, from PODEMOS in Spain, Syriza in Greece and the Labour Party in the UK, with its leader, Jeremy Corbyn, proposing his own 21st century socialism model for the country. As such, it represents perhaps the most important political challenge to the status quo anywhere in the world.

Neoliberalism is dying. In recent times we have seen the rise of huge political movements due to the negative impacts of neoliberal policy, both on the right (like those around Donald Trump and Marine Le Pen) and on the left (like Bernie Sanders and Jeremy Corbyn). However, this wave started in Latin America, and in Venezuela more specifically, as the region was the "Empire's Workshop", where these theories, and their negative consequences were first seen (Grandin, 2006). Long before the Seattle World Trade Organization protests in 1999 Venezuela was electing a leader promising to end the neoliberal experiment. This gives understanding Venezuela a special importance, as the country is years ahead of us in the neoliberal cycle, so studying it can give us an understanding of where our own societies may go in the future.

And yet the media themselves have been accused of being the chief ideological weapon in manufacturing consent for neoliberalism and elite views more generally (Gramsci, 1971; Herman and Chomsky, 1988), with studies showing it presents the ideology as common sense and does not treat alternative ideas about society as credible (Berry, 2016).

Therefore, two questions arise when thinking about the media and Venezuela:

1 How has the Western press covered the country since 1998: what themes consistently arise, what positions do the media take on key issues and where do they fall on the spectrum of opinions on the country?
2 Why is it covered this way: what factors influence the output of the Western media?

This book is split into two parts. Part I (Chapters 1–5) answers the first question and is based upon a sample of 501 newspaper articles from seven of the most influential English-language newspapers on the subject across the time period 1998–2014. Part II (Chapters 6–8) explores the second question, primarily through interviews with 27 journalists and academics covering the country.

Although this study deals with how the media portrays only one country, it has a much broader resonance. If neoliberalism is dying, what will replace it? If the media treat Venezuela, one prominent alternative to neoliberalism poorly, how will they treat a Corbyn government or Sanders presidency in the future? It also gets to the heart of the nature of contemporary media and how they operate. As such, this study actually tells us much more about our own media than about Venezuela.

The media and Latin America

The media has enormous power in shaping public opinion. As Bagdikian (1992: preface, 26) said, it is:

> The authority at any given moment for what is true and what is false, what is reality and what is fantasy, what is important and what is trivial. There is no greater force in shaping the public mind.

Therefore, the impact the media has in shaping debates about our future society is immeasurable.

The radical Italian academic Antonio Gramsci (1971) argued that it was not primarily by force that a small elite at the top held power over society, but through the process of *hegemony*, whereby the elites use schools, churches, and, crucially for this study, the media, to *manufacture consent* among the population for their rule, attitudes, outlooks and taste.

Exploring this idea more fully, Herman and Chomsky (1988) posited that news is systematically distorted to reflect the interests of state and corporate power. The media's societal purpose therefore is to manufacture consent for the elite's decisions. In *Manufacturing Consent*, the authors attempt to explain how public opinion is manipulated through the five systematic biases, or "filters", the for-profit, private media have. These five filters are:

1 Elite ownership of the media, whether through single media barons or through a large group of wealthy shareholders;
2 Reliance on advertising from big businesses as the primary means of income;
3 Reliance on official sources, credible 'experts' and government officials;
4 Flak, negative responses to media that have the effect of chiding journalists into compliance with the 'official' line;
5 Anti-socialism, how any organization or government Western governments label as 'communist' or 'socialist' will be attacked (1988: 2).

Today, six multi-billion dollar corporations control the majority of what Americans see, hear and read. These are, in order of gross revenues, Comcast, Disney, News Corporation (Murdoch), Time Warner, Viacom and CBS. There exists a similar situation in the United Kingdom. Just three corporations, News UK (Murdoch), DMGT and Trinity Mirror control 70 percent of newspaper circulation (Media Reform Coalition, 2014). Furthermore, for all the talk of new media, the majority of the most frequently visited news websites in the UK and USA are the online arm of the dominant national news corporations. One owner controlling such a great amount of our media has profoundly negative effects on the state of democracy and the breadth of information and views the public are exposed to. Many owners closely control the content of their newspapers. For example, in 2014 it was widely reported a Scottish National Party leader met Rupert Murdoch in order to convince him to support Scottish independence. Taken as a given was Murdoch's ability to change the editorial stances of all his media (Monbiot, 2014).

While today media is less likely to be owned by press barons and more likely to be a corporation owned by thousands of anonymous shareholders, it is no less problematic. Corporate shareholders have no interest in the veracity of the news, only in short-term profits. Furthermore, media corporations have become vast conglomerations with interests in many different sectors. For instance, at the time of the invasion of Iraq, *NBC* was owned by General Electric, a huge weapons producer who stood to make massive profits from the war. *NBC* supported the invasion uncritically. Editors and managers are aware that their prime responsibility is to increase profit for shareholders, and it is unclear why journalists should see themselves as working for a different company to workers on an assembly line in the weapons factory. Are news corporations to be trusted to impartially report on Venezuela when some have considerable interests there?

Advertising is crucial in shaping the content of news. Today, the vast majority of funding for private, for-profit newspapers comes in the form of advertising, and only a small minority through the purchases of copies. This jumps to 100 percent for free newspapers and much television, radio and online content. This has serious consequences for the content of media; Bagdikian (1992: 121) lamented that advertising revenues have "insulated these media from the wishes of their audiences". Large corporations insist that the content of the media does not share a contrary message to that of the advertisement. Thus, articles inviting the reader to think critically are discouraged and those that would promote an ideology other than neoliberalism are extremely rare. Advertisers constantly interfere in the content of news. A recent example was the reaction of advertisers to *The Guardian* after it broke the Edward Snowden NSA spying revelations. Although the huge news event drew massive numbers to the newspaper, it also led to advertisers pulling out of the company, a key factor in the decline of the newspaper's American operation. As one former executive said, "While Snowden put us on the map, it makes corporate clients very nervous about wanting to get big into *The Guardian*" (Perlberg, 2017). Journalists must understand and imbibe the message from the companies who pay their salaries: do not challenge corporate profits. Given that the Venezuelan government is challenging not only corporate profits but the entire system of neoliberalism, it is unsurprising to see highly negative coverage.

Today, journalists are instructed to try not to take sides in arguments themselves, instead to leave opinions to others and simply stick to reporting facts. Journalists are strongly encouraged to find credible, official sources to quote, often from the government, think tanks, business leaders or university professors. They must therefore carefully cultivate elite contacts. If they reflect critically on what their sources are telling them or report the news in a manner that contradicts the official line, they risk angering the source and run the possibility that the source will refuse to speak to them again. Unfortunately, the outcome of this is frequently simply a parroting of official positions across the media. Veteran journalist Robert Fisk (2013) explained the problem:

> I'm just looking at a copy of the Toronto *Globe and Mail*, February 1st, 2013. It's a story about al-Qaeda in Algeria. And what is the sourcing? 'US intelligence officials said', 'a senior US intelligence official said', 'US officials said', 'the intelligence official said', 'Algerian officials say', 'national security sources considered', 'European security sources said', . . . We might as well name our newspapers 'Officials Say'. This is the cancer at the bottom of modern journalism, that we do not challenge power anymore.

Whether it comes from the government, businesses, pressure groups or other sources, flak can have the effect of chiding journalists into compliance with the dominant line. It can take many forms, including letter writing campaigns, lawsuits or smear campaigns.

Finally, the anti-socialist filter has the effect of tarring journalists arguing against the conservative consensus as untrustworthy, anti-American or traitorous. By this mechanism, journalists can be chided into producing more conservative content.

Herman and Chomsky used their model to compare elections in the left-wing controlled Nicaragua to those in El Salvador and Guatemala. They characterize the process in the latter two countries as undertaken under severe and ongoing state terror while contrasting it with the relatively free and fair Nicaraguan elections. Nevertheless, they found the US media were sympathetic to the Guatemalan and Salvadorian governments while adopting a combative line against Nicaragua because the *right* people won in Guatemala and El Salvador and the wrong ones (those hostile to US corporate interests) won in Nicaragua.

Studying the media's coverage of Nicaragua, as well as in Chile under the socialist government of Allende (1970–1973) and Brazil under the progressive liberal Goulart (1961–1964), Parenti found similar demonization of any forces not conducive to American state and corporate interests, concluding that there are four rules that govern Western media coverage of left-wing countries:

1 An absence of any positive comments on democratic or economic reforms;
2 Sympathetic portrayal of the rich suffering oppression, unless it is possible to find oppressed poor;

3 A silence on the negative effects of US policy and violence in the region;
4 Build up an image of economic adversity due to mismanagement of the economy that is inherent to socialism (1993: 186).

Academic analysis of the media's coverage of Venezuela has begun to emerge (see Bhatt, 2013; Delacour, 2005; Chernomas and Hudson, 2012). While insightful, all these studies have been limited latitudinally (only looking at one or a few media sources in one country) or longtitudinally (looking at only one specific event). This study analyzes a wide range of Western media's portrayal of the country across the entire *chavista* period (1998–present) and fills that gap.

A short primer on Latin American history

Soon after Columbus first set foot on the Paria Peninsula in Venezuela in 1498, Latin America became a slave plantation society, where small numbers of white Iberians enslaved larger numbers of indigenous Americans and sub-Saharan Africans to produce primary products like sugar and coffee for the European market. By slavery's abolition in 1797, some 100,000 Africans had been brought to the country. Venezuela, like much of Latin America, achieved its independence in the early half of the 19th century when disgruntled creole (American-born) elites, who had been shut out of political power, turned to nationalism. However, after independence, the basic structure of the economy and society did not change. Latin American countries still produced primary products for export and imported finished goods, meaning they were heavily dependent on the rich countries.

Venezuela's liberator was Simon Bolivar, a charismatic army officer who led a number of heroic campaigns to drive the Spanish out of South America. Bolivar argued that the fledgling independent states could only achieve true independence through unity, otherwise the United States, the new power in the region, was "destined to plague Latin America with misery under the guise of liberty". Bolivar managed to unite Venezuela, Ecuador, Colombia, Panama, along with parts of Peru, Brazil and Guyana into a united state. In fact, Bolivia was named in his honour. To this day, Ecuador, Colombia and Venezuela are considered sister countries and share near identical national flags. However, regional differences quickly tore the country apart and a dejected Bolivar gave up, stating that "America was ungovernable" and that "those who serve the revolution are ploughing the sea".

Bolivar's predictions proved prescient, as the US came to dominate the region it called its "backyard". Throughout the 20th century, the

US helped overthrow democratically elected governments in Latin America, replacing them with often vicious dictatorships that suited American business interests, for example in Guatemala in 1953, Chile in 1973 and Honduras in 2009. This has left many in Latin America feeling that its vast wealth is not going towards helping the people.

Venezuela under Chavez was the first country in a new wave of governments that came to power wishing to fulfill Bolivar's dream of unity and challenge what they saw as US imperialism. By 2011, the large majority of South American countries had elected left-of-centre governments who began to establish themselves as independent actors, offering asylum to Western dissidents like Chelsea Manning, Edward Snowden and Julian Assange and moving away from close relationships with large international banks like the US-based IMF. Together, these countries founded new international organizations to further advance Bolivar's goal of a united, independent Latin America, like the Bank of the South, CELAC, an alternative to the US-dominated Organization of American States (OAS) and even a common currency.

The United States has not given up control over the region, however, and has continually sought to produce regime change in Venezuela and many of its neighbours. The ascendance of Trump signals a heightened tension between the two countries, with the President opening discussing military invasion.

Compared to many of its neighbours, late 20th century Venezuela was considered a relatively stable democracy. Yet by the 1980s, the country was suffering a severe economic crisis. In 1989, Carlos Andres Perez was elected President on an expressly anti-neoliberal platform. However, within weeks he implemented a wide-ranging austerity and privatization programme that made matters worse. Perez ordered the army to crush the protests to his programme, which led to a massacre of thousands.

Poverty, inequality, unemployment and inflation hit crisis points, as corrupt officials made fortunes from selling off collectively owned property. Perez was impeached but the situation became worse. Hugo Chavez, an army officer who had shot to prominence attempting to overthrow Perez, campaigned on an anti-corruption platform that argued the country needed a new constitution. The political outsider was shockingly elected President in 1998, leading to a debate around the meaning of democracy (see Chapter 1). He was re-elected in 2000 with a huge majority. However, the elites, who had shared power since 1958, tried to overthrow him in 2002, only for it to be beaten back spectacularly by one of the largest demonstrations of people power from the poor majority of working-class Venezuelans (see Chapter 2). They tried many more times to unseat him, including a business lockout between 2002 and 2003 but could not do so, and Chavez died in 2013, undefeated and was replaced by his hand-picked successor, Nicolas Maduro (see Chapters 3–4). Since Chavez's death, Venezuela has gone through another protracted economic crisis. The opposition saw this as a chance to force Maduro out, trying in 2014 (see Chapter 5) and again in 2017. However, it has not yet been able to take power back.

Chavez was the first non-white President in the majority non-white country's history. Since the times of slavery, where whites were landowners and blacks and Amerindians were slaves, Venezuela has been a highly racially and socially unequal country. There still persists a high correlation between class and race today, with the white elites the descendants of the Spanish landowners. The elite of the country live Westernized lives at Western standards while working-class Venezuelans struggle in poverty (see Chapter 6). Darker skinned Venezuelans were functionally barred from well-paid jobs in the oil industry, adding to the race/class dimension. The poor are mostly black and the black are mostly poor. There is a strong correlation between race, class and voting tendencies inside Venezuela (Cannon, 2008). Chavez, a mix of Amerindian and African, drew his support from the lower classes of Venezuelans who saw for the first time a President that looked and talked like they did. Half of those voting for him in 1998 had never voted before. They lived in adobe huts in the countryside like the one Chavez had grown up in or in the *barrios*, the overcrowded slums of the major cities, synonymous with poverty and crime.

The polarization between those who oppose and those who support the government is made worse by the intense racial and class segregation of Caracas. Much of the elite live inside private gated communities in Eastern Caracas protected by armed guards. Chacao, on the east side, is home to the headquarters of international businesses, Ferrari dealerships and some of the most expensive private schools in Latin America. It is also where virtually all Western journalists live and work. Property values are some of the highest and poverty levels are some of the lowest in Latin America. Therefore, those who live there rarely come into contact with the poor majority of Caracas residents who live precarious existences in the shantytowns on the hills surrounding the city. This is a problem as there is a lack of integration and communication between rich and poor. This is compounded by the high crime rates in the city, which further dissuade travel into less luxurious areas. Therefore, journalists who live in Chacao are effectively living in a socially-constructed bubble of privilege and rarely see the other side of life. This is explored more fully in Chapter 6.

Oil was discovered in Venezuela 100 years ago and has become by far the most important industry in the country – both a blessing and a curse. Venezuela has the largest proven oil reserves in the world, equal to Iraq, Libya, Qatar, Algeria, Azerbaijan, Oman, Egypt, Yemen, Syria and Bahrain *combined* (OPEC, 2014). Between the 1970s and 1990s, at the behest of the US, it overproduced oil, undermining the OPEC cartel and keeping prices very low. This changed completely with Chavez, who reinvigorated the cartel, cutting back on production. As a result, the price of oil rose from $9 per barrel in 1999 to over $140 in 2008. He also renationalized the oil industry, reducing profits for Western multinationals and angering the US government. These geopolitical tensions will be explored in Chapter 8.

Methodology

This study uses a mixture of quantitative and qualitative methods, combining the strengths of both, to produce accurate and generalizable data. The quantitative method is content analysis, where occurrences of specific phenomena are counted, in order to highlight clear trends within the reporting. The primary qualitative method used is a modified thematic analysis. Thematic analysis was developed by the Glasgow University Media Group (GUMG), and posits that on any controversial issue there will be a number of competing arguments and explanations. The first step is to identify the range of understandings being put forward to produce a "conceptual map" of the spectrum of beliefs on any issue. News media is then analyzed to show how often each side's arguments are referenced or highlighted. The method has become a staple of analyzing news media and has been used to explore how the media have covered a number of controversial issues, such as the miner's strike, the financial crisis and the Israel/Palestine conflict.

In addition to highlighting the competing arguments and explanations, this study will provide the reader with the best empirical data available to further inform their understanding of the topic. This data will come in the form of population surveys and reports from organizations like the World Bank and United Nations. Combining these two methods will allow for both in-depth and generalizable research.

In order to fully explore the first question of how the Western media cover Venezuela since 1998, it is necessary to include a wide range of newspapers from both sides of the Atlantic and to cover the entire *chavista* period (1998–). Thus, seven of the most influential newspapers from both sides of the Atlantic, from both the left- and right- wing were studied. They were *The New York Times, The Washington Post, The Miami Herald, The Guardian, The Times, The Daily Telegraph* and *The Independent*.

The articles were selected from peak periods of interest. They were the 1998/99 election and inauguration of Chavez, the 2002 coup attempt, Chavez's 2013 death and the subsequent election of Nicolas Maduro and the 2014 demonstrations against the government. Any relevant article from the Nexus database with the word "Venezuela" appearing in these newspapers anywhere in the text was analyzed. This produced a dataset of 501 articles. There were 232 articles from left-of-centre publications, 229 from right-wing sources and 40 from centrist newspapers. Therefore, trends found in the sample can be said to represent a wide range of Western opinion over a long period of time. The results of this are presented in Chapters 1–5.

In order to best explain the second question of why Venezuela is covered in the way it is, 27 interviews were conducted with journalists and academics covering the country. The list of those participating and their position at the time of the interview is as follows:

Anatoly Kurmanaev, a Caracas-based journalist for *Bloomberg*,

Brian Ellsworth, a journalist in Venezuela since 2002, working for *Reuters*,

Girish Gupta, a freelance journalist in Caracas who has written for *The Guardian, The New York Times, USA Today* among others,

Jim Wyss, Andean correspondent, *The Miami Herald*,

Sibylla Brodzinsky, a journalist in Bogota covering Venezuela for *The Guardian*,

Bart Jones, former *Los Angeles Times* journalist who spent eight years in Venezuela,

Matt Kennard, fellow of the Centre for Investigative Journalism who covered Venezuela for *The Financial Times*,

Steve Ellner, Professor of Economic History at the Universidad de Oriente, Venezuela,

Rick Rockwell, Associate Dean, School of Communications, Webster University,

Francisco Toro, prominent Venezuelan opposition blogger and former journalist at *The Washington Post, New York Times, Financial Times* and *The Guardian*,

Dan Beeton, economist and International Communications Director and the Center for Economic and Policy Research, Washington, D.C.,

Kurt Weyland, Professor of Latin American Politics, University of Texas,

Michael Derham, Senior Lecturer in Spanish, Northumbria University,

Julia Buxton, Professor of Comparative Politics and Associate Dean for Academic Affairs and Programs at Central European University, Budapest,

George Ciccariello-Maher, Assistant Professor of Political Science at Drexel University,

Ian Hudson, Associate Professor of Economics at the University of Manitoba,

Jairo Lugo-Ocando, former Chief News Editor of Venezuelan newspaper *La Verdad* and Lecturer in Journalism Studies at the University of Sheffield,

Joe Emersberger, blogger on the media and Venezuela at *Spinwatch* and writer for Venezuelan media channel, *TeleSur*,

Keane Bhatt, activist and writer for the North American Congress on Latin America,

Lee Salter, Lecturer in Media and Communication at the University of Sussex,

Michael Parenti, lecturer and author of "Inverting Reality: the Politics of News Media",

Pascal Lupien, Research Enterprise and Scholarly Communication Librarian, University of Guelph, Ontario,

Dr. Kevin Young, formerly of Stony Brook University and a specialist in applied media theory in South America,

Justin Delacour, Adjunct Assistant Professor, Pace University,

John Pilger, veteran journalist for *The Guardian* and *The Daily Mirror*,

In addition, there were other journalists who agreed to be interviewed on condition of anonymity. They were:

Journalist 1, a journalist in Caracas for an American newspaper;
Journalist 2, a Venezuelan journalist working for a Western news organization.

The first chapter deals with how the media covered Chavez's 1998 election and inauguration.

References

Bagdikian, B. (1992) *The Media Monopoly*, Boston: Beacon Press.

Berry, M. (2016) "No Alternative to Austerity; How HHC Broadcast News Reported the Deficit Debate," *Media, Culture & Society*, 38:6, pp. 844–863.

Bhatt, K. (2013) "The Hypocrisy of Human Rights Watch," *NACLA Report on the Americas*, 46:4, p. 55.

Cannon, B. (2008) "Class/Race Polarisation in Venezuela and the Electoral Success of Hugo Chavez: A Break With the Past or the Song Remains the Same?" *Third World Quarterly*, 29:4, pp. 731–748.

Chernomas, R. and Hudson, I. (2012) *The Gatekeeper: 60 Years of Economics According to The New York Times*, London: Paradigm.

Delacour, J. (2005) "The Op-Ed Assassination of Hugo Chavez," *Fair.org*, http://fair.org/extra-online-articles/the-op-ed-assassination-of-hugo-chvez/7/?issue_area_id=9

Fisk, R. (2013) " 'We Might as Well Name Our Newspapers' Officials Say,' " Interview on *Democracy Now*, May 7th, www.democracynow.org/2013/5/7/robert_fisk_on_syrias_civil_war?autostart=true

Gramsci, A. (1971) *Selections From the Prison Notebooks*, London: Lawrence and Wishart.

Grandin, G. (2006) *Empire's Workshop: Latin America, The United States, and the Rise of the New Imperialism*, New York: Metropolitan Books.

Herman, E. and Chomsky, N. (1988) *Manufacturing Consent: The Political Economy of the Mass Media*, New York: Pantheon.

Media Reform Coalition (2014) "The Elephant in the Room: A Survey of Media Ownership and Plurality in the United Kingdom," www.mediareform.org.uk/wp-content/uploads/2014/04/ElephantintheroomFinalfinal.pdf

Monbiot, G. (2014) "How the Media Shafted the People of Scotland," *The Guardian*, September 16th, www.theguardian.com/commentisfree/2014/sep/16/media-shafted-people-scotland-journalists

OPEC (2014) "OPEC Annual Statistical Bulletin 2014," *OPEC*, www.opec.org/opec_web/static_files_project/media/downloads/publications/ASB2014.pdf

Parenti, M. (1993) *Inverting Reality: The Politics of News Media*, New York: St. Martin's Press.

Perlberg, S. (2017) "How the Guardian Lost America," *Buzzfeed*, June 21st, www.buzzfeed.com/stevenperlberg/how-the-guardian-lost-america?utm_term=.spAB1d1D4#.uaDmyRy7Z

Walser, R. (2010) "State Sponsors of Terrorism: Time to Add Venezuela to the List," *The Hertiage Foundation*, January 20th, www.heritage.org/research/reports/2010/01/state-sponsors-of-terrorism-time-to-add-venezuela-to-the-list

Part I

1 The election of Hugo Chavez, 1998–99

A threat to democracy?

Venezuelan history 1958–1998

After the downfall in 1958 of the strongman Marcos Perez Jimenez, Venezuela was ruled for 40 years by two parties: AD and COPEI. That year, the two parties signed a pact at the residence of Rafael Caldera in Punto Fijo, agreeing to a political alliance and to share power between themselves. The period has since become known as the *Punto Fijo* period.

There has been much debate about the nature of the system these parties installed. Presented here are the three dominant strains.

Venezuelan exceptionalism

In contrast with other Latin American countries, late 20th century Venezuela was often seen as a beacon of stability and democracy. Unlike neighbours such as Colombia, Venezuela was not wrecked by widespread civil war, and in comparison to much of Latin America, ruled by military dictatorships, Venezuela had all the formal institutions of democracy. This, it is argued, made it an exception to the norm and immune to the region's chronic social and political ills. Many claimed the strength of AD and COPEI blocked a slide into dictatorship (Levine, 1977), that oil wealth reduced tensions and increased stability (Karl, 1987) and that high levels of political participation demonstrated the strength of Venezuelan democracy (Martz, 1984).

However, this narrative was interrupted in the 1980s and 1990s, which brought with it economic disaster, massive drops in living standards, vastly increased inequality and a massive government massacre of thousands of protestors (thereafter known as the *Caracazo*). The Venezuelan exceptionalism thesis therefore became largely obsolete in academia, with even some of its chief defenders, such as Levine (1994), rethinking their previous positions.

Revisionist histories

Revisionist historians claim that the democracy Venezuela enjoyed was a minimalist version, limited to electoral activity and individual rights. Furthermore, the *Punto Fijo* pact was not only inclusionary, but also exclusionary, as it specifically excluded some widely supported parties from holding office. Revisionists argue while Venezuela did enjoy a golden period in the 1970s, the fissures in the surface began to show in the 1980s and exploded in the succeeding decade. Indeed, many academics refused to classify it as a democracy any more, preferring terms such as "partyarchy" or "polyarchy" (Hellinger, 2011: 30) to define the system.

Buxton (1999, 2001) argued that during the *Punto Fijo* period, Venezuelan institutions' neutrality was fundamentally undermined by the corrupt system of partyarchy, where the two major political parties controlled virtually every appointment. She argues that the military, the judiciary, the state administration and electoral bodies were subject to intense politicization, with appointments dependent on party contacts, and that elections were hopelessly rigged. Civil society organizations such as unions or NGOs would be brought into the partyarchy system by plying them with money, while elections were rigged. They were able to afford bribery on a vast scale by making sure to siphon off state funds into the parties. And no one would testify or rule against them as the top judges were all AD or COPEI loyalists. Thus, Buxton concluded that AD and COPEI "constantly conspired against the expression of the popular vote through gerrymandering, vote stealing and intimidation" and "political institutions had no credibility" with the population (1999: 180–181).

The radical critique

Buxton argued that Venezuela by 1998 had rotted to the core, but others have put forward an even harsher critique: that Venezuela was an entirely undemocratic police state. Ciccariello-Maher (2013: 10) categorizes the *Punto Fijo* period as:

> An attack on the people, as a subversion of the popular will that had ousted the dictator, and as an effort to prevent the incursion of the people into the halls of official power . . . at the very heart of Venezuela's so-called democracy a veritable conspiracy against the pueblo.

Concentration camps existed in the country (Ibid: 51), and Wilpert (2011) alleges that thousands of political opponents were tortured and disappeared, culminating in the crescendo of violence that was the *Caracazo* of 1989. This school argues it is only in the context of economic meltdown and brutal repression that we can understand the rapid rise of the political outsider Chavez.

Chavez was elected on the promise to found a new constitutional convention in order to clean up the rampant corruption in the state's institutions and found a new republic. Supporters argued that this was a necessary move in improving democracy. Critics claimed this was a sign of creeping authoritarianism. As this chapter will show, the media has largely sided with the critics.

Empirical evidence

Empirical data suggests that virtually every post in liberal institutions before 1998 was attained due to party loyalty rather than merit. A 1992 report by the World Bank concluded that the judicial system was in crisis due to excessive politicization and bureaucratic incompetence. A UN survey stated that the Venezuelan judiciary was one of the "least credible in the world" (Buxton, 2001: 32). The appointment of judges was done officially through a quota system, with AD and COPEI appointing officials from their own parties to the judiciary. This led to a situation where clientalism, incompetence and fraud reigned.

President Carlos Andres Perez himself admitted fraud in Venezuela was "like a bad African country", which rendered democracy "an embarrassment" (Ibid: 92). The media was completely politicized and tied to the two major parties. Television stations were shut down and President Perez established state censors in every newsroom in the country (Jones, 2008: 163). Elections themselves were rigged in favour of AD and COPEI. In 1993, it was found that many dead people had "voted" for those parties. Catedral District, for example, had 4,000 inhabitants according to records but 16,000 people voted form there that year (Buxton, 2001: 88). When all else failed, AD and COPEI colluded to steal votes for third parties and share them between themselves (Ibid: 94–99). A leaked instruction manual to AD supporters told them to "distract officials with violence" on election day and to "try and alter the ballot, particularly the vote of organizations with no witness" (Ibid: 93).

Empirical evidence gathered from Latinobarómetro (1995–2015), a strongly anti-*chavista* (Young, 2014) polling organization show that

Venezuelans themselves believe the country's democracy and its institutions were extremely flawed in the 1990s but improved to become
the best democracy in Latin America by Chavez's death in 2013. When
asked on a scale of 1–10 how democratic their country was, Venezuelans in 1997 gave a mixed response, the most common answer being
five, with only 13 percent responding that the country was fully democratic. By 2013, by far the most common answer was that Venezuela
was a perfect democracy, with 29 percent of the population agreeing,
the highest in Latin America.

Venezuela's attitude to its democracy is mirrored by their opinion
about their democratic institutions. In 1996, fewer than 3 percent had
a lot of confidence in political parties, with nearly two-thirds professing no confidence whatever in them. By 2013, 16 percent now had a lot
of faith, with less than one-third having none, among the best figures
in Latin America. Trust in the public administration as a whole grew
by over 300 percent between 1996 and 2013 to become the highest in
Latin America, double that of the second highest country. Trust in the
judiciary doubled between 1996 and 2013, with those professing a lot
of confidence in it jumping from 9.6 percent to 18.5 percent. Although
that figure appears low, it is second highest in Latin America, behind
only Costa Rica. Confidence in the police more than tripled between
1996 and 2013 too. In 1997, 11 percent of Venezuelans believed elections were clean, with 83 percent believing them to be fraudulent. By

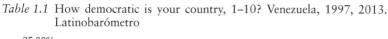

Table 1.1 How democratic is your country, 1–10? Venezuela, 1997, 2013.
Latinobarómetro

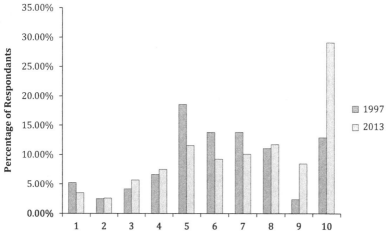

Table 1.2 Venezuelan elections: clean or rigged? 1997 and 2006, Latinobarómetro

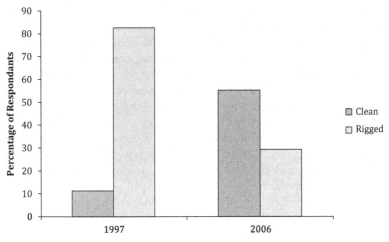

2006, despite the media claiming constantly they were rigged, 56 percent believed them clean, with only 30 percent agreeing with the media (for more on elections and the media, see Chapter 4).

When allowed to speak for itself, the data shows Venezuelans believe the country suffered a profound democratic deficit before Chavez, but that his government, although there remained problems, had made significant, if not enormous improvements to it. Thus, presenting the *Punto Fijo* period as a democratic era and Chavez's "Bolivarian Revolution" as a regression into tyranny would be completely contrary to the empirical evidence. However, as we shall see, the media portrayed the country in exactly this fashion. Empirical evidence presented throughout this book comes from the most respected sources and is easily available online in English. As such, they would be the first places a journalist would go to find quotable statistics for reporting. Journalists were well aware of these polls, as they frequently cited the data, but to present a totally contrasting picture of the country.

Analysis

A sample was taken of all relevant articles featuring the word "Venezuela" anywhere in the text. The seven newspapers used throughout this study are *The Guardian*, *The Times*, *The Daily Telegraph*,

The Independent, The New York Times, The Washington Post and *The Miami Herald*. There were four sample periods: 1998–9, 2002, 2013 and 2014. However, data from the 1998–9 sample discussed this question far more frequently than the other years. The sample dates for this period were between September 1st, 1998 and March 1st, 1999, covering Chavez's election campaign and inauguration. The exception was *The Miami Herald*, where the dates December 1st to December 8th were used. This was done in order to make sure the newspaper, which publishes far more Venezuelan stories, did not overwhelm the sample.

The newspapers presented the *Punto Fijo* period (1958–1998) quite differently, many framing it as a model democratic era that was undermined with the election of Chavez, whose government set about destroying and politicizing once neutral and efficient democratic institutions. While there was a deal of critical reflection on the previous period, particularly from UK articles, there was little to no sense that the government had actually improved matters. Indeed, the opposite was usually alleged.

It may have been expected there would be a good deal of critical reflection of the period, considering in 1998 the two-party system, thought by many to be exemplarily stable, was comprehensively ended with the landslide election of a jailed outsider who promised to destroy it and build a new republic. Overall, the *Punto Fijo* period was identified 38 times as a good democracy and 41 times as being undemocratic or seriously flawed. The British papers were far more likely to reflect on the period negatively, framing it positively eight times while framing it negatively 15 times.

A typical description of the problems of the system was found in *The Independent* (1998):

> Added to that is the widespread feeling that Mr Caldera's government has hovered between inept and corrupt.

In contrast, the American media were more likely to present the state of affairs as democratic:

> Venezuelan business leaders and foreign investors will be watching closely to see whether his moves mirror the campaign rhetoric that raised questions about his commitment to free markets – and to the country's 40-year democratic tradition.
>
> (*The Washington Post*, 1998a)

Table 1.3 Newspapers' identifications of the *Punto Fijo* system

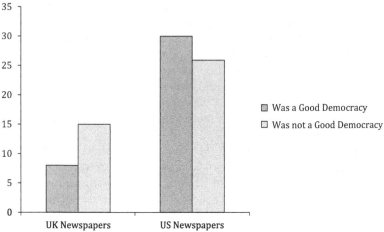

Indeed, even years after Venezuelan exceptionalism became considered obsolete in academia, newspapers continued presenting the period as a golden age of democracy. For example, in an editorial in 2013, *The Miami Herald* (2013a) wrote:

> For Venezuelans, the choice is clear: They can move forward, restoring the democracy that Venezuela once was, or they can watch their country continue to deteriorate under a Chávez apprentice like the official candidate, Nicolas Maduro.

Political institutions

Some historians criticize the *chavistas* for undermining democratic state institutions like the police and judiciary, while others claim they are building bottom-up, more democratically run alternatives to these, challenging the ideas that these institutions were exemplary and independent of political control at all before Chavez.

In total, there were 56 articles presenting the *chavista* government as destroying Venezuelan institutions whereas there were eight articles referencing the government building better, more representative institutions than before. While already skewed, this number makes the imbalance appear less pronounced than it is. All eight came from the 1998–1999 sample and most allusions to this idea were claims by

Table 1.4 Newspaper articles on Venezuelan institutions

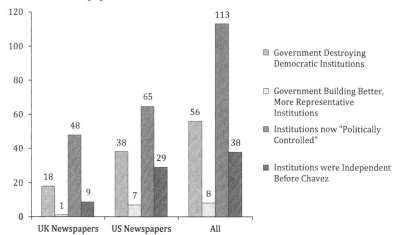

Hugo Chavez himself, whom the newspapers already took a skeptical view of. A typical example of this was the following:

> Chavez has vowed to call a referendum on dissolving Congress and creating a constituent assembly that he says would be more representative of the people and an effective weapon in the fight against corruption.
>
> (*The Washington Post*, 1998b)

From 1999 to 2014 there was no positive discussion of the radical experiment in participatory democracy in Venezuela, which had drawn great interest from academics (Lievesley and Ludlum, 2009; Sitrin and Azzelini, 2014) and where the government claimed it was attempting to empower its own citizens to take control over decisions to do with their own lives. This is exactly in line with Parenti's four rules on how the media portray leftist Latin American countries (see introduction). However, throughout the entire sample there was a good deal of condemnation of how the government was destroying democratic institutions of Venezuela. This was common in both UK and US newspapers.

The Independent (2002) claimed that Chavez:

> Did not live up to early constitutional promises on human rights and the rule of law. Vast powers were shifted to the presidency,

state institutions were packed with supporters, and opponents were harassed and imprisoned.

The tone in the American papers was more negative. *The Washington Post* (2013) summed up what newspapers had been accusing Chavez of for years:

> How are liberal institutions destroyed? These days, no military coup is necessary. Instead, cynical and determined rulers [like Chavez] aim to corrupt rather than abolish independent courts, legislatures and media – and their defenders are too divided, too weak or too distracted to respond effectively.

These particular explanations led to many articles (113) arguing that Venezuelan institutions were now politically controlled. The opposing viewpoint, that these institutions have always been politically controlled, only that now they are controlled by the *chavistas*, was virtually absent. The *chavista* notion that the institutions are independent was completely absent. Indeed, many articles, nine in the UK and 29 in the US, insinuated that institutions were highly professional and completely politically independent before Chavez's rise – something which contradicts the empirical evidence. Thus, the courts, which, in 1996 Latinobarómetro showed less than 10 percent of Venezuelans had a good deal of faith in, and which Buxton (1999, 2001) showed were filled with judges appointed solely on the basis of what party they belonged to were presented as previously "bastions of judicial independence" only now "packed" with *chavista* judges (*The Miami Herald*, 2013b).

Even before he gained office, *The Washington Post* (1998c) was warning that Chavez might destroy institutions' independence:

> Several administration officials said they feared Chavez would attempt to use his broad support for fighting corruption to assume near dictatorial powers, curtailing freedom of expression and the independence of the courts, as Peruvian President Alberto Fujimori did.

The newspapers in the survey showed a tendency to present the pre-Chavez period as a democratic era while presenting Chavez as a threat to that democracy, somebody who was undermining the neutrality and independence of democratic institutions such as the courts and the police. They rarely discussed the alternative opinion that there was a radical experiment in a much deeper, meaningful and participatory democracy under way inside the country. This is particularly problematic as empirical data taken from organizations with an anti-*chavista* bias show that not only was there low or extremely low confidence in elections, democratic institutions and the government in the country pre-1998, but that during the Chavez period those confidence levels rose to become some of the highest, if not the highest, in Latin America. Thus, readers were given only one opinion on the matter and were not informed of the radical democratic experiment that had generated a huge increase in interest in the country around the world. Furthermore, the one opinion that readers were exposed to is contradicted by empirical evidence. It is this context in which the rest of the book should be understood.

References

Buxton, J. (1999) "Venezuela," in Buxton, J. and Phillips, N. (eds.) *Developments in Latin American Political Economy: States, Markets and Actors*, Manchester: Manchester University Press.

Buxton, J. (2001) *The Failure of Political Reform in Venezuela*, Aldershot: Ashgate.

Ciccariello-Maher, G. (2013) *We Created Chavez: A People's History of the Venezuelan Revolution*, Durham: Duke University Press.

Hellinger, D. (2011) "Chavismo and Venezuelan Democracy in a New Decade," in Smilde, D. and Hellinger, D. (eds.) *Venezuela's Bolivarian Democracy: Participation, Politics, and Culture Under Chavez*, Durham: Duke University Press.

The Independent (1998) "Venezuelan Coup Leader 'to Win Poll,'" December 3rd.

The Independent (2002) "An Era of Grand Political Illusion Comes to an End," March 7th.

Jones, B. (2008) *Hugo! The Hugo Chavez Story From Mud Hut to Perpetual Revolutionary*, London: Vintage.

Karl, T. (1987) "Petroleum and Political Pacts: The Transition to Democracy in Venezuela," *Latin American Research Review*, 22:1, pp. 35–62.

Latinobarómetro (1995–2015) *Latinobarómetro Reports*, www.Latinobarómetro.org/

Levine, D. (1977) "Venezuelan Politics: Past and Future," in Bond, R. (ed.) *Contemporary Venezuela and Its Role in International Affairs*, New York: New York University Press, pp. 7–44.

Levine, D. (1994) "Goodbye to Venezuelan Exceptionalism," *Journal of Inter-American Studies and World Affairs*, 36, pp. 145–182.

Lievesley, G. and Ludlum, S. (eds.) (2009) *Reclaiming Latin America: Experiments in Radical Social Democracy*, London: Zed Books.

Martz, J. (1984) "Venezuela, Colombia, and Ecuador," in Black, J. (ed.) *Latin America: its Problems and Its Promises*, Boulder: Westview Press, pp. 381–401.

Miami Herald (2013a) "Venezuela's Chance to Move Forward," April 11th.

Miami Herald (2013b) "Democracies Should Support Demand for Recount in Venezuela," April 16th.

Sitrin, M. and Azzelini, D. (2014) *They Can't Represent Us: Reinventing Democracy From Greece to Occupy*, London: Verso.

Washington Post (1998a) "Venezuela's Chavez Faces High Hurdles," December 7th.

Washington Post (1998b) "Chavez Victory Called Democratic Revolution," December 9th.

Washington Post (1998c) "U.S. Warns Incoming Venezuelan President," December 10th.

Washington Post (2013) "The End of a Freedom Fighter?" March 4th.

Wilpert, G. (2011) "How Venezuela's Right Discovered Human Rights," *NACLA Report on the Americas*, 44:5 (September-October), pp. 29–36.

Young, K. (2014) "Democracy in Latin America: The Results of the 2013 Latinobarómetro Public Opinion Poll," *Venezuelanalysis*, January 2nd, http://venezuelanalysis.com/analysis/10262

2 The 2002 coup

On April 11th, 2002, a coup deposed Chavez, replacing him with businessman Pedro Carmona. While in power, Carmona decreed several notable things. He abolished the recently ratified constitution, suspended the Supreme Court, liquidated Congress and gave himself the power to rule alone with a council of advisors. He also changed the name of the country. Hundreds of people from the top of society signed Carmona's decree, legitimizing the events.

However, Carmona's government lasted less than 48 hours, as huge counter-demonstrations from Venezuela's dark-skinned working classes encouraged loyal troops to retake the Miraflores presidential palace and oust him. Nineteen people were killed and 69 wounded on April 11th, with twice as many *chavistas* killed or wounded than opposition demonstrators (Wilpert, 2007).

Three key points of contention have been identified in which there are competing explanations:

1 Was this a coup or a popular protest?
2 What was the extent of United States involvement?
3 What was the extent of the local media's involvement?

During the hectic events of April, there were two main explanations for the affair that journalists could draw upon. One framed the events as a patriotic uprising against a repressive regime. This was the position espoused by the US government and the Venezuelan media. The second posited that this was a coup orchestrated by the Venezuelan elite. This viewpoint was expressed by both the Venezuelan government and international organizations like the OAS.

Competing explanations

The uprising narrative

On April 12th, the International Republican Institute (IRI), a semi-official US government body "applauded the bravery" of civil society leaders who peacefully "restored genuine democracy" to Venezuela by removing Chavez from office, its President, George Folsom (2002) stating (emphasis added):

> Last night, led by *every sector of civil society*, the Venezuelan people *rose up to defend democracy* in their country. Venezuelans were *provoked* into action as a result of *systematic repression by the Government of Hugo Chavez*. Several hundred thousand people filled the streets of Caracas to demand the resignation of Lt. Col. Hugo Chavez. Chavez responded with sharpshooters and his paramilitary Bolivarian circles killing more than 12 civilians and wounding more than 100 others. In contrast, IRI commends the patriotism of the Venezuelan military for their refusal to fire on their countrymen.

The White House used almost identical language (Fleischer, 2002). However, after the coup was beaten back, questions about the US' role began to emerge, to which a government spokesperson emphatically insisted:

> The United States did not participate in, inspire, encourage, foment, wink at, nod at, close its eyes to, or in any way leave the impression that it would support a coup of any kind in Venezuela. The record is crystal clear.
>
> (Gutierrez, 2002)

Indeed, the government claimed it had put "intense pressure" on Carmona to abide by democratic norms (Ibid).

The coup thesis

Despite the US and Colombian governments pressuring other Latin American states to recognize Carmona immediately, the OAS condemned the events and expressed solidarity with the Venezuelan people (Office of the Inspector General, 2002: 78). At around 3.30 am on the morning of the 12 April, Environment Minister Ana Elisa Osorio announced to journalists that Chavez had refused to resign and that this was a *coup d'état*. Other senior *chavista* politicians did the same. Osorio urged the journalists to "let the world know" (Jones, 2008: 39). They did not. Indeed, the *chavistas* claim that their point of view was consciously censored from virtually all Venezuelan media and that they did not have any outlet for the truth, as the coup-plotters had shut down state media. However, international satellite media broadcast statements from Chavez's family and the President of Cuba giving their explanations of the events. General Jorge Garcia stated that the media were not courageous, but were an intimate part of the conspiracy, campaigning for a coup in an "openly fascist" campaign (Chavez and Guevara, 2006: 131).

The *chavistas* claimed the coup was reversed due to the courageous uprising of millions of ordinary Venezuelans who came down from the hills to protest. This was accomplished despite the best efforts of opposition mayor Leopoldo Lopez, who Garcia charges closed off traffic tunnels to stop the counter-coup (Chavez and Harnecker, 2005: 131).

Therefore, these two frames of understanding could hardly differ more greatly. One charges that the events were a patriotic uprising against a tyranny, while the other frames it as another American-backed right-wing coup in Latin America.

The uprising frame is not at all popular in academia (Wilpert, 2009), with most of even the strongest critics of Chavez agreeing that the events constituted a coup (see Corrales and Penfold, 2011: 22; Carroll, 2013: 2; Marcano and Barrera Tyszka, 2007: 167). However, some claim there is still some ambiguity to who was responsible for the shooting (Marcano and Barrera Tyszka, 2007: 168–188, Corrales and Penfold, 2011: 22) and to the level of US involvement (Carroll, 2013: 82). Others take US involvement and opposition culpability as a given (Ciccariello-Maher, 2013: 170–175).

Empirical evidence

American government documents later obtained under the Freedom of Information Act confirm both US involvement and the level of planning the opposition put into the coup. The documents prove that many of the coup's leaders, such as Pedro Carmona and Leopoldo Lopez, travelled multiple times to Washington to visit the IRI and top Bush administration officials (Golinger, 2007: 44–49). The National Endowment for Democracy (NED) and USAID had been funding a wide range of anti-government groups who planned the coup, and funding for their activities quadrupled in 2001.

The documents show that, by at latest March 5th, the US government was aware that those it was funding were about the overthrow Chavez. The US did not warn him, but instead quadrupled its funding *again* in 2002.

Table 2.1 NED and USAID grants to Venezuelan organizations, 2000–2006, Golinger (2007: 56)

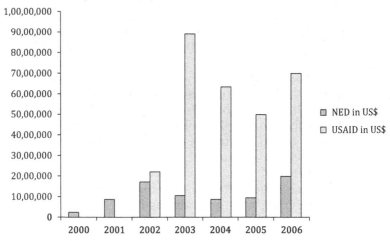

A "top secret" April 6th cable headlined "Conditions Ripening for Coup Attempt" said:

> Dissident military factions, including some disgruntled senior officers and a group of radical junior officers, are stepping up efforts to organize a coup against President Chavez, possibly as early as this month.
>
> (Ibid: 64)

It went on to note that opposition figures would provoke violence in order to arrest Chavez. It also commented on the level of detail of their plans, confirming that it had seen them. Therefore, the US government incontrovertibly knew that a coup was planned for early April by opposition figures they had been funding and flying to Washington for meetings for months and that they would try to provoke and exploit violence from demonstrations against the government. It should be noted that the documents have been heavily redacted in order to prevent information the US government does not want others to know from being made public.

Furthermore, on 11 April, the US Ambassador, Charles Shapiro was at the mansion of Gustavo Cisneros, the headquarters of the coup (Jones, 2008: 319) while top officials like Otto Reich were in regular contact with Cisneros by telephone (Livingstone, 2011: 32–33). US military officers were present at the barracks where Chavez was sent, and two US ships entered Venezuelan territory and made for the remote island of La Orchila, where he was later helicoptered to. After the coup, the US doubled its funding to the same groups that had organized the coup, continuing to fly coup-plotters like Maria Corina Machado to the White House at taxpayer expense. In short, there is ample evidence of US involvement in the coup.

The role of the media

The Venezuelan media is characterized by its extreme concentration and its strong opposition to Chavez. Virtually all the private stations were owned by multi-millionaires with close ties to the opposition. It was no accident that the coup's headquarters were at media baron Gustavo Cisneros' mansion. Cisneros was the richest man in Venezuela and a close friend of the Bush family (Kozloff, 2007: 68). The vast majority of the media strongly supported the coup, demanding that Venezuelans overthrow the government. *El Nacional*, one of Venezuela's most influential newspapers told its readers to "take to the streets, not one step backwards!" and celebrated the coup's apparent success with a special edition and the front page headline proclaiming "A Step Forward!"

Many television channels broadcast calls for an insurrection and broadcast doctored images of *chavistas* under attack to make it seem as if they were the aggressors, images used to justify intensifying the coup.

On 11 April, Vice-Admiral Hector Ramirez was invited on Cisneros' Venevisión. He thanked the media for their indispensable help, saying "We had a deadly weapon: the media. And now that I have the opportunity, let me congratulate you" (Lemoine, 2002). The morning after Chavez was ousted, influential journalist Napoleon Bravo invited some of the ringleaders on his show, *24 Hours*. One stated that "we were short of communications facilities and I have to thank the media for their solidarity and cooperation" (Jones, 2008: 343). Bravo also hosted other top coup leaders like Leopoldo Lopez and Rear Admiral Carlos Molina, who confided that they had been planning it for over a year (Wilpert, 2007).

TV stations broadcast coup-leader Antonio Ledezma's decree that over 200 pro-government figures were to be rounded up while a purge of over 500 journalists considered politically dubious took place (Dominguez, 2011: 120–121). The private media joined in the witch-hunt, helping to hunt down journalists, trade unionists and politicians (Jones, 2008: 349). In less than a day, over 100 were imprisoned (McCaughan, 2004: 93) while others were tortured or publicly flogged (Ciccariello-Maher, 2013: 170). Media sympathetic to the Chavez administration were closed, forced off the air and ransacked.

As the counter-coup grew, the media refused to cover it, instead showing Julia Roberts movies alongside generals announcing Chavez had resigned. A director of RCTV later said his orders were "zero *chavismo* on screen" (Ibid: 174). *CNN* correspondent Otto Neustadt testified that on April 10th he was told that the next day there would be shootings at the protests and that dozens of military officials would appear on television to denounce the government. He subsequently recorded these opposition figures' condemnations *before any violence had taken place*, strongly implicating the opposition for the killings.

Analysis

A sample of all relevant articles featuring the word "Venezuela" was taken for the dates January 1st 2002 to June 1st 2002, excepting *The Miami Herald*, where, due to the quantity of articles, the dates April 1st to May 1st were used. This produced a total of 133 articles.

In the wake of what appeared a successful coup attempt, all the newspapers published editorials on the nature of the Chavez administration; they were, in effect, political obituaries. For example, *The New York Times* (2002a) emphatically endorsed the events, even claiming no coup took place, stating (emphasis added):

> With yesterday's *resignation* of President Hugo Chavez, Venezuelan democracy is no longer threatened by a would-be dictator. Mr. Chavez, a ruinous demagogue, *stepped down* after the military intervened and handed power to a respected business leader, Pedro Carmona.

Every newspaper published content strongly supporting the coup. *The Times* (2002a) claimed Chavez was a mass murderer, stating that few Venezuelans mourned his end, but they did mourn his victims, "demonstrators gunned down by his snipers yesterday before the presidential palace", and it published an article from sitting UK government minister Denis MacShane, who called Chavez a "ranting, populist demagogue" (2002b). Many of the newspapers justified the coup by claiming Chavez had alienated the entire country, as can be seen from the following passages:

> Chavez has managed to alienate almost every sector of Venezuelan society.
>
> (*The Guardian*, 2002a)

Chavez managed to alienate just about everybody in the country, including business, the media and the trade unions, with his weird mixture of fascism, populism and anti-globalisation.

(*The Daily Telegraph*, 2002a)

When these articles were written, Carmona had just liquidated the courts, the constitution, the parliament, declared himself autocrat, and the opposition had just ordered the arrest of politicians, activists and journalists. However, according to *The Telegraph*, Chavez, who won numerous clean elections, was the "fascist". Evidently, Chavez had not alienated most of society, as his return, where large numbers of dark-skinned working-class Venezuelans rose up, attests. The language used bears a stark resemblance to the previously noted statement by George Folsom of the IRI and of the White House, suggesting close ties between big media, the CIA and the White House. Meanwhile, as he was announcing himself as dictator, Carmona was portrayed overwhelmingly positively (an over 3:1 ratio), as a safe pair of hands, a "soft-spoken civic leader" (*The Miami Herald*, 2002a) and as a "level-headed" and "meek" "conciliator" (*The New York Times*, 2002b).

A coup or not a coup?

In total, there were 164 different identifications of the events of April 2002 as a coup and 166 categorizations of the events as not a coup, where words such as "resignation", "fall" or "affair" were used. Indeed, *The New York Times* had a series of articles in April entitled "Uprising in Venezuela", which connotes a very different set of circumstances and respectability to the word "coup". However, there was a marked difference between the likelihood of British and American newspapers to identify the affair as a coup, with *The New York Times* most likely to frame the events as an uprising. But all newspapers carried articles that stated that what occurred was not a coup.

The Miami Herald wrote that "what began as a strike by oil workers early last week exploded into a full-fledged popular uprising" (2002b) that ousted Chavez after "he assumed de facto dictatorial powers, cutting off television signals and allowing his followers to fire on protesters" (2002c). Indeed, one *Herald* article (2002d), while giving space to one of the coup leaders to directly deny any coup was taking place at all, reminded readers *on three separate occasions* that Hugo Chavez attempted a coup in 1992.

Table 2.2 What happened in Venezuela? 2002 newspaper identifications

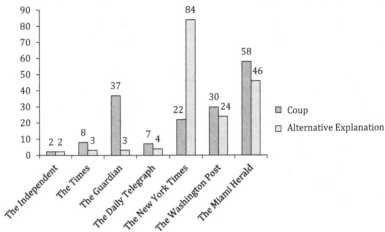

However, it was *The New York Times* (2002c) that showed by far the greatest propensity to frame the events as a popular uprising that Chavez was "toppled by popular protests" that he "sought to contain with force that led to bloodshed" leading to his downfall and that the phenomenon has "been hailed as a refreshing manifestation of democracy".

Thus, the narrative, particularly from *The New York Times*, was that spontaneous popular protests against an enraged Chavez led him to order his forces to shoot on the crowd, prompting the military to force him to resign – *exactly* the same position as the US government. This was despite the fact that the newspapers knew a coup was imminent, as they had been reporting on it for months. *The Washington Post* (2002a) reported that the US House of Representatives were even publicly debating the imminent coup themselves. The coup was the worst kept secret in Venezuela. As *The Miami Herald* (2002e) reported, "Rumors of a coup to oust Chavez were being whispered, if not shouted, for months before the revolt."

On April 15th, White House spokesperson used the word "coup" for the first time. After that time there was a marked increase in the use of the word from *The Washington Post*, again suggesting a convergence. However, even weeks after the events, *The New York Times* preferred to use alternative explanations such as "unrest", "popular uprising" or "Hugo Chavez's temporary downfall".

When the word "coup" was used, it was frequently mentioned as an accusation from an already discredited source. For instance, *The New*

York Times (2002d) reported that, "The television broadcasts angry statements by pro-Chavez officials charging that he was forced out of power in a coup orchestrated by the elite."

Consider the four following sentences about weapons of mass destruction (WMDs):

> "There were no WMDs in Iraq."
> "The UN stated there were no WMDs in Iraq."
> "Saddam Hussein claimed there were no WMDs in Iraq."
> "Mass-murdering dictator Saddam Hussein angrily insisted that, despite many allegations to the contrary, there were no WMDs in Iraq."

All four are factual statements. But each statement carries a very different level of believability. Newspapers in the sample often undermined contrary arguments by presenting facts as accusations; accusations made by officials the newspapers had spent years demonizing. Similarly, allegations against the government were either stated as fact or quoted from sources the newspapers gave the reader no reason to doubt, even when their reliability was highly questionable.

US involvement in the coup?

In total, 12 of 31 UK articles and 11 of 112 US articles entertained the possibility that the United States Government was in any way connected to the 2002 coup. But only *The Guardian* presented US involvement as a strong possibility.

In contrast, many articles specifically asserted that Washington was not involved, thus arguing against a virtually unstated opponent. *The Washington Post* claimed (2002b):

> Both the Clinton and Bush administrations chose to ignore most of Mr. Chavez's frequent provocations; there's been no suggestion that the United States had anything to do with this.

The Daily Telegraph (2002a) went out of its way to argue against an unstated opposing view in its editorial on the subject, applauding Washington's policy of "masterly inaction":

> Anticipating correctly that the Chavez government would *fall of its own accord*, like a rotten fruit. The last thing the Americans need is a new set of *myths* about Yanqui coup-mongering, after

Table 2.3 2002 articles mentioning possible US involvement in the coup

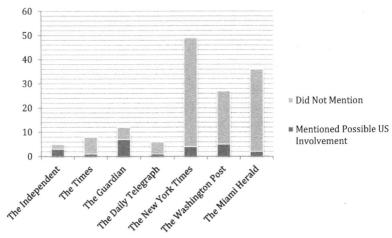

the fashion of their alleged role in the overthrow of Chile's Salvador Allende in 1973.

(emphasis added)

Thus, on the question of US involvement, the media took exactly the same position as the US government. If there was no question of US involvement, the question remains unanswered as to why the media chose to specifically reject this, rather than, for instance, Swedish involvement.

When US involvement was considered, it was often immediately brushed off. *The Independent* (2002) noted (emphasis added):

Some *cynics* even pointed to the hand of the CIA while world attention was on the Middle East conflict. The US reaction to the violence, though, has been muted.

The Daily Telegraph (2002b) noted that, "Iran, Iraq and Cuba were among the countries that welcomed Mr Chavez's restoration yesterday, claiming that the coup was a US plot."

It should be pointed out that these were counted as references to possible US involvement. The three countries mentioned were considered rogue dictatorships at the time in the US and UK. Thus, the newspaper simultaneously represented the Chavez government as a friend of dictatorships and the notion of US involvement as something believed only by the likes of Saddam Hussein and Ayatollah Khamenei. It did not note that the countries of the Organization of American States, such as Brazil or Mexico, also welcomed the return of the constitutional order.

The New York Times had still milder criticism of the US government. A week after the coup, when reports of the aforementioned actions of the White House and US military had been published, *The New York Times* (2002e) did note:

> Some critics have judged that the US was too quick to accept reports of the resignation of President Hugo Chavez and too slow to defend the democratic system that elected him.

Other critics judged that the US government had actively planned and carried out a coup d'état against an elected head of state that left nineteen dead, but those critiques were not published. Weeks after the coup, *The New York Times* (2002f) conceded that, while not a coup and while not involved, the US Government "appeared to endorse" the new government while *The Washington Post* (2002c) noted the Bush administration "appeared to send" a message of support for the coup although previously noting that "few Latin American officials appeared to believe the United States was involved", (2002d). The Bush administration "appeared to send" that message by strongly supporting the coup internationally and pressuring other countries into doing the same.

However, *The Guardian* was interested in the idea of the United States' involvement in the coup, publishing articles on the subject. It catalogued how the US Government pressured Latin American diplomats at the OAS to accept the coup (2002b) and Charles Shapiro's actions on the day of the coup (2002c).

Media involvement in the coup?

As noted before, the Venezuelan media were a central component of the coup; indeed, its involvement could hardly have been more important and conspicuous.

Of the 139 articles in the 2002 sample, seven mentioned possible media involvement.

However, Duncan Campbell in *The Guardian* was the only journalist to base a story on the media's involvement in the coup, noting that the media "certainly played a major part" (2002d) collaborating with the coup plotters, then imposing an information blackout once Chavez supporters rallied to take back the palace (2002e).

Table 2.4 2002 articles mentioning media involvement in the coup

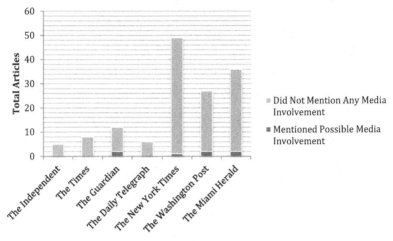

In contrast, *The New York Times* addressed the reality of the media's involvement only once, and only as an accusation made by Chavez, who the outlet had labeled "authoritarian", a "ruinous demagogue", a "would-be dictator" and "incompetent" in recent days, thereafter proceeding to present evidence against that charge. The article noted that the reason for the blackout was the following:

> For journalists, maligned by Mr. Chavez's verbal attacks and attacked by the president's supporters, the decision not to publish or broadcast was clear-cut: either go home or face possible death in streets teeming with armed men.
>
> (2002g)

It did not note that the media had been happy to not only publish the previous days, where 19 people had been shot dead, but to participate in and lead a coup and help the Carmona government attack, imprison and torture other journalists who did not share their ideology.

To conclude, many editorials in the wake of Chavez's apparent demise made clear that the editorial boards approved of the overthrow of an elected head of state and of his replacement with Carmona as a step forward for democracy. Chavez and his supporters were slandered with potentially highly libelous misrepresentations about their actions. And yet no apologies were forthcoming and, to this day, the inaccuracies stand uncorrected. In situations where news media make serious errors in reporting, it is customary to issue apologies. It is a similar practice in diplomacy. Instead, both the US government and the newspapers issued statements hoping that Hugo Chavez would henceforth rule in a less autocratic manner. The majority of the media closely mirrored the positions of the US government on all the key issues, not only in tone and substance, but even in wording. The lack of apologies afterward, recognizing their errors in the fog of war, is hard to reconcile with the idea that the media attempted to report the coup accurately and honestly.

References

Carroll, R. (2013) *Comandante: The Life and Legacy of Hugo Chavez*, London: Cannongate.

Chavez, H. and Guevara, A. (2006) *Chavez, Venezuela and the New Latin America: An Interview With Hugo Chavez by Aleida Guevara*, New Delhi: Leftword Books.

Chavez, H. and Harnecker, M. (2005) *Understanding the Venezuelan Revolution: Hugo Chavez Talks to Marta Harnecker*, New York: Monthly Review Press.

Ciccariello-Maher, G. (2013) *We Created Chavez: A People's History of the Venezuelan Revolution*, Durham: Duke University Press.

Corrales, J. and Penfold, M. (2011) *Dragon in the Tropics: Hugo Chavez and the Political Economy of Revolution in Venezuela*, Washington, DC: Brookings Institution.

The Daily Telegraph (2002a) "Venezuela's Bad Apple," April 13th.

The Daily Telegraph (2002b) "Venezuela President Swept Back to Power," April 15th.

Dominguez, F. (2011) "Venezuela's Opposition: Desperately Seeking to Overthrow Chavez," in Dominguez, F., Lievesley, G. and Ludlum, S. (eds.) *Right-Wing Politics in the New Latin America: Reaction and Revolt*, London: Zed Books.

Fleischer, A. (2002) "Ari Fleischer Briefs Reporters," *CNN*, April 12th, http://edition.cnn.com/TRANSCRIPTS/0204/12/bn.14.html

Folsom, G. (2002) "IRI President Folsom Praises Venezuelan Civil Society's Defense of Democracy," April 12th, www.prnewswire.com/news-releases/iri-president-folsom-praises-venezuelan-civil-societys-defense-of-democracy-76942222.html

Golinger, E. (2007) *The Chavez Code: Cracking US Intervention in Venezuela*, London: Pluto Press.

The Guardian (2002a) "Chavez Rises From Very Peculiar Coup," April 15th.

The Guardian (2002b) "US 'Gave the Nod' to Venezuelan Coup," April 17th.

The Guardian (2002c) "American Navy 'Helped Venezuelan Coup,'" April 29th.

The Guardian (2002d) "G2: The Coup," April 22nd.

The Guardian (2002e) "Media: It's a Coup: Your Sets Will Adjust Accordingly," April 29th.

Gutierrez, L. (2002) "Venezuela's Uncertain Future: Challenges for U.S. Policy," *U.S. Department of State Archive*, April 17th, http://2001-2009.state.gov/p/wha/rls/rm/9573.htm

The Independent (2002) "Army Topples Venezuelan President After 13 Killed," April 13th.

Jones, B. (2008) *Hugo! The Hugo Chavez Story From Mud Hut to Perpetual Revolutionary*, London: Vintage.

Kozloff, N. (2007) *Hugo Chavez: Oil, Politics, and the Challenge to the U.S.*, New York: St. Martin's.

Lemoine, M. (2002) "Venezuela's Press Power," *Le Monde Diplomatique*, August, http://mondediplo.com/2002/08/10venezuela

Livingstone, G. (2011) "The United States of America and the Latin American Right," in Dominguez, F., Lievesley, G. and Ludlum, S. (eds.) *Right-Wing Politics in the New Latin America: Reaction and Revolt*, London: Zed Books.

Marcano, C. and Barrera Tyszka, A. (2007) *Hugo Chavez*, translated by Kristina Cordero, New York: Random House.

McCaughan, M. (2004) *The Battle of Venezuela*, London: Latin American Bureau.

Miami Herald (2002a) "Venezuelan Defends his Brief Presidency," April 20th.

Miami Herald (2002b) "Business Owners Lament Their Losses in Weekend Looting," April 17th.

Miami Herald (2002c) "Chavez Turmoil a Blow to Latin American Populism," April 14th.

Miami Herald (2002d) "Venezuela in Crisis After Deadly March," April 12th.

Miami Herald (2002e) "Venezuelan Defends His Brief Presidency," April 20th.

New York Times (2002a) "Hugo Chavez Departs," April 13th.

New York Times (2002b) "Man in the News; Manager and Conciliator- Pedro Carmona Estanga," April 13th.

New York Times (2002c) "The Continent; A Vicious Circle: Failures and Instability," April 13th.

New York Times (2002d) "Behind the Upheaval in Venezuela," April 18th.

New York Times (2002e) "Man in the News; Combative Point Man on Latin Policy," April 18th.

New York Times (2002f) "U.S. Hasn't Kept Promise to Latin America, Critics Say," May 19th.

New York Times (2002g) "Venezuela Press Sidestepped Leader's Return," April 23rd.

Office of the Inspector General (2002) "A Review of U.S. Policy Toward Venezuela November 2001–April 2002," United States Department of State, https://oig.state.gov/system/files/13682.pdf

The Times (2002a) "No Bolivar," April 13th.

The Times (2002b) "I Saw the Calm, Rational Chavez Turn Into a Ranting, Populist Demagogue," April 13th.

Washington Post (2002a) "Political Crisis in Venezuela Worries White House," February 23rd.

Washington Post (2002b) "Venezuela's Breakdown," April 13th.

Washington Post (2002c) "Chavez Raises Idea of U.S. Role in Coup," May 5th.

Washington Post (2002d) "Bush Officials Defend Their Actions on Venezuela," April 18th.

Wilpert, G. (2007) "The 47 Hour Coup That Changed Everything," *Venezuelanalysis*, April 13th, https://venezuelanalysis.com/analysis/2336

Wilpert, G. (2009) "The Venezuelan Coup Revisited: Silencing the Evidence," *NACLA Report on the Americas*, 42:4 (July-August).

3 Hugo Chavez's death and funeral

Competing opinions on Chavez's legacy

President Chavez died on March 5th, 2013. A common theme throughout this study is the extreme divergence of opinion on matters relating to Venezuela. Above all, this is the case when discussing his legacy. Did Chavez's "Bolivarian Revolution" leave Venezuela and its society better or worse off?

Critical opinions

Weyland (2013) claimed Chavez's legacy was that he "slowly and surely smothered democracy", maintaining a façade of democracy while entrenching authoritarian rule and "unfettered control" over all walks of society in order to "limit debate, strike at their opponents, and drastically tilt the electoral playing field". Toro (2013) took a still more critical line, claiming Chavez "wasn't just a zany buffoon, he was an oppressive autocrat" who destroyed freedom of speech, and created a brainwashed population in a society where "an off-the-cuff remark could land you in jail". Carroll (2013: 232–233) compares Chavez unfavourably with Kim Jong-Il and claims he employed "virtual slaves" in his social programs (Ibid: 220). He portrays his economic legacy as one of decay, where Venezuela, led by a "disastrous manager", "peeled, chipped and flaked into moneyed dysfunction" (Ibid: 215–216), suffering crippling food shortages (Ibid: 206–213).

Anderson (2013) characterized his economic legacy as one "defined by confiscation, expropriation, governmental incapacity, and the use of violence" presenting Chavez as a "slumlord" who destroyed the lives of Venezuelans. Others (Plummer, 2013) claim Chavez destroyed the Venezuelan economy through unsustainable public spending, leading to crippling inflation.

Supportive voices

In contrast, Unite (2013), Britain's largest union, released a statement that read:

> Hugo Chavez and the Bolivarian Revolution have been a massive inspiration for all those engaged in the fight for social justice and who believe that another world is possible.

It went on to say, "under Chavez's leadership Venezuela has been transformed beyond recognition for the better". Dangl (2013) claimed that Chavez's social programs in health, housing, education and food had drastically improved the lives of most Venezuelans and that the *chavistas* had created "some of the most sophisticated and successful experiments in direct democracy". Duno-Gottberg (2013) claimed that the most telling characteristic of the revolution was that it was so popular that the opposition felt compelled to mimic Chavez and pretend to be centre-leftists. Others have claimed that Chavez presided over and "economic miracle" (Sirota, 2013) where Venezuela went "from bust to boom" (Buxton, 2013), enjoying high growth and low unemployment in a virtual golden age for the country.

As with all questions on Venezuela, there is no agreement. Therefore, the aid of empirical data would be greatly helpful.

Empirical data

The empirical data presented comes from the most unimpeachable sources available, such as the United Nations and World Bank. All of the data presented is also fully and easily available in English to anyone with a computer. Thus, it should be the first port of call for journalists. The data covering the legacy of the Bolivarian Revolution has been split up into two sections: social and economic. The indicators presented below were chosen because they are among the most common indicators used to judge a country's progress and because they were the issues most frequently brought up in the newspapers themselves.

Social indicators

The Human Development Index (HDI) is the UN's flagship statistic in measuring social wellbeing. It combines economic data with other factors, such as medical and education levels to produce a number reflecting the development of a society. All countries have a number between zero (completely undeveloped) and one (completely developed). With a score of .942 in 2012, Norway was the world's most developed country (UNDP, 2015). With a score of 0.348, Niger is one of the world's least developed countries.

In the 20 years between 1980 and 2000, Venezuela increased its HDI value from 0.628 to 0.673, an increase of 0.045. However, in the 10 years of *chavista* rule between 2000 and 2010, its score rose to 0.757, an increase of 0.084, almost twice the increase in development in half the time. This was achieved in spite of the opposition's 2002/3 lockout/strike, which took a severe blow on the economy, shrinking it by one third in a few months, sharply decreasing the HDI score. Under the Chavez government, Venezuela improved from "medium human development" to "high human development" (UNDP, 2013).

UN statistics show the number of children enrolled in secondary school increased from under one half in 1999 to nearly three-quarters in 2012 (CEPALSTAT, 2016a). The country now has one of the world's largest student populations, despite being home to only 30 million people. It was programs such as these which academics supportive of the administration claim led to a sense of empowerment an awakening in the Venezuelan population. In 2005, UNESCO, an agency of the UN declared Venezuela illiteracy free.

Both poverty (49.4%) and extreme poverty (17.9%) peaked in Venezuela in 1999, after 10 years of neoliberalism and the year Chavez took office. By 2012, poverty (25.4%) had been reduced by half and extreme poverty (7.1%) by three-quarters (CEPALSTAT, 2016a). However, some observers sympathetic to Chavez have noted that the poverty reductions include only monetary poverty, and do not take into account the gains in health, education and other social progress (Weisbrot and Sandoval, 2007).

A report published by the UNDP (2010) showed a steep increase in the number of calories available for Venezuelans between the late 1990s and 2010. In 2013, the UN's Food and Agriculture Organization (FAO) gave the country a special commendation for its exemplary work reducing malnourishment. The FAO also noted that the number of undernourished Venezuelans was 2.8 million between 1990 and 1992, rose to 3.8 million between 2000 and 2002 and fell to a "not statistically significant" number by 2010 to 2012. In 2013 the FAO (2013) calculated that there were 3,020 calories available per person per day in Venezuela, a figure much larger than the 1,800 per person per day it recommends as a minimum and far larger than the figure of under 1,800 available in 1999 when Chavez became

Table 3.1 Venezuela: poverty and extreme poverty, 1990–2012 ECLAC, 1990–2013

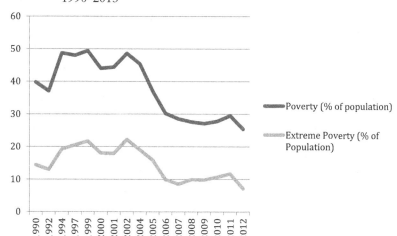

President. Indeed, the FAO (2013) warned that Venezuela's most pressing food problem might now be obesity, which affected 38 percent of the population.

However, violent crime rose significantly in Venezuela during the 2000s, from 25.0 intentional homicides per 100,000 inhabitants in 1999 to 53.6 in 2012 (World Bank, 2016), making Venezuela among the most dangerous countries in the most dangerous region in the world for homicides. Furthermore, the violence is largely localized to the *barrios*, the shantytowns in the hills of the city while less than one percent of the homicides occur in the wealthy Chacao district (Humphrey and Valverde, 2014: 157). Therefore, Venezuelans' experiences of violent crime differ greatly along class and geographic lines. In Chapter 6, journalists interviewed expressed fear for their safety because of high crime rates.

Economic indicators

GDP per capita is the benchmark statistic for measuring the health of the economy. Data from the World Bank (2016) show that Venezuelan GDP per capita rose from $5150 dollars in 1999 to $6434 in 2012, in spite of the opposition's 2002–3 strike/lockout. After the government gained control over the oil industry in 2003, the economy fared well. The figures show that economic growth under Chavez was markedly superior to growth under the two previous, neoliberal presidents, Caldera and Perez. According to the UN, unemployment in Venezuela fell from 15.0 percent in 1999 to 8.1 percent, despite the strike/lockout, which caused countless businesses to permanently close and unemployment to soar (CEPALSTAT, 2016c). Inflation was brought under control by the Chavez administration. Indeed, the highest annual inflation under Chavez was around equal to the lowest rate of annual inflation under the previous two (neoliberal) presidents, Caldera and Perez.

Inequality, as measured by the GINI index, fell considerably, with Venezuela's GINI score falling from 0.498 in 1999 to 0.405 in 2012 (ECLAC, 2013: 91; World Bank, 2016). By 2012, Venezuela was the second most equal country in Latin America, behind only Uruguay. UN data shows that the poor saw their share of national income rise, the poorest 40 percent's share rising from 14.3 percent of national income in 1999 to 19.8 percent in 2013, a rise of over a third. The bottom 70 percent increased their share of the national income. This was done without financially hurting the middle classes as we have seen that GDP rose substantially under the Chavez administration. Their share of national income dropped marginally, from 29 to 28 percent under Chavez. However, the growing economy meant their total income was much higher in 2012 than in 1999. It was only the richest 10 percent of Venezuelan society who were financially worse off under Chavez (ECLAC, 2013: 89).

Table 3.2 Venezuela: share of income by class, 1990–2012, ECLAC (2013: 89)

As can be seen on the graph, there was no great revolution in income inequality. Rather, a slow but significant transferal of income from the richest 10 percent to the lower 70 percent of society.

Overall, the data show considerable social and economic progress under Chavez, with inequality, poverty, illiteracy, malnourishment and inflation falling greatly while GNP per capita and human development increasingly substantially. However, despite the rhetoric of some *chavistas*, there was no economic revolution. Nor was Venezuela transformed into a model economy. Unemployment and inflation fell considerably, but remained high. Furthermore, violent crime increased greatly and the country was still dependent on oil revenue for income, something that would cause a deep recession after Chavez was gone.

Analysis

A sample was taken of all relevant articles in the seven newspapers with the word "Venezuela" in the text. The sample dates were between March 1st and May 1st, 2013. The exception was *The Miami Herald*, where, in order to stop the newspaper overwhelming the sample, the weeks March 1st-8th and April 11th-18th were chosen. These dates still covered Hugo Chavez's death and funeral and the following presidential elections, and were therefore the peak period of interest. The two 2013 periods were analyzed together but split up for the sake of convenience of reading.

In Western countries like the United Kingdom and the United States, there is a strong cultural practice of not speaking ill of the dead, particularly the recently deceased. Thus, obituaries of public figures tend to be markedly positive, celebrating people for their qualities and downplaying or ignoring their faults. So strong is this custom that even extremely negative traits of characters are referred to with euphemistic compliments. It is custom to describe boring people as "tireless raconteurs", drunkards as "vivacious", while "he tended to become over-attached to certain ideas and theories" is used as a euphemism for "fascist" (Ferguson, 2002).

This custom is illustrated with the obituaries of King Abdullah of Saudi Arabia, who died in January 2015. Saudi Arabia under Abdullah was one of the world's worst human rights abusers, with Human Rights Watch's (2013) report noting many of the country's nine million workers suffer in "slavery-like conditions", where freedom of religion is banned and where Abdullah personally ordered the public crucifixion of children who supported the Arab Spring online.

British Prime Minister David Cameron (2015) claimed he was "deeply saddened" by his death, noting he would be remembered for "his commitment to peace and for strengthening understanding between faiths." It is illegal to practice any religion but that of Abdullah's and apostates are regularly sentenced to death. President Obama (2015) noted his warm friendship with Abdullah and characterized him as a peacemaker and an educator.

The media observed this custom in their obituaries. *The Washington Post* and *The Independent* (2015) described Abdullah as "a shrewd ruler who was popular with his subjects", while *The Daily Telegraph* (2015) noted he "become known as something of an advocate for women". *The New York Times* (2015) noted that his greatest legacy would be a scholarship that sends tens of thousands of young Saudi men to study at Western universities. Thus, even in extreme circumstances, such as the death of the head of a regime dubbed one of the most oppressive in world history, the custom of not speaking ill of the dead held.

The reaction from much of the world to Chavez's death was deep sadness. The President of Bolivia broke down and cried on television as he said that his country was "destroyed" by it but noted that "Chavez is alive more than ever", and that he "will remain an inspiration to the peoples struggling for liberation" against the United States (*El Universal (Colombia)*, 2013).

President Correa of Ecuador called Chavez:

> A great Latin American, a great human being" who "the whole world will recognize for greatness and courage . . . those who die for life cannot be said to be dead. Hugo Chavez died for the life of his beloved Venezuela, for the life of a unified Latin America. He will be more alive than ever.
>
> (Kozameh, 2013)

The governments of Brazil, Peru, Haiti, Ecuador, Argentina, Chile, Uruguay and the Dominican Republic all took the step of declaring three days national mourning. Nicaragua and Bolivia declared a week, Cuba two days, and Surinam one day. More countries declared national mourning after Chavez's death than after Nelson Mandela's.

In South Africa, President Zuma of South Africa claimed Chavez was a "visionary" and "respected revolutionary leader of . . . the entire progressive family of nations" (*Times Live*, 2013). Meanwhile President Abbas of Palestine claimed his people would "be forever grateful to Chavez" for his "courageous support" (*TeleSur*, 2015).

Given that Hugo Chavez was not accused of anything approaching the crimes of Abdullah, it would be expected to find similar praise and sadness in his obituaries. However, that was not the case.

The Times (2013a) presented Chavez to its readers as a dogmatic, violent narcissist who had a "fascination with the sound of his own voice" and "went out of his way to attack . . . business leaders, bankers, newspaper owners, trade union bosses . . . even the Catholic Church". In a separate article that day, it presented Chavez as a buffoon, full of "idiotic bombast" and suffering from a "Christ complex" (2013b).

Diagnosing Chavez from afar with mental disorders was something the newspapers regularly did throughout the sample. *The Independent* (2013a) quoted a psychiatrist who diagnosed Chavez as a "narcissist", "impulsive", "temperamental" and "hypersensitive to criticism".

The Daily Telegraph (2013a) noted he was a "shrewd demagogue" who "combined brash but intoxicatingly rhetorical gifts with a free spending of oil revenues" which "failed to create and upsurge in employment", and described him as a man who "went out of his way to pick fights" with the US and other Venezuelan groups. As seen previously, UN figures show unemployment halved under Chavez, from 15 percent in 1999 to 8 percent in 2012. It also portrayed Chavez as uncouth lout, claiming he was "no intellectual", despite the fact that Chavez was a university lecturer before becoming president, this position often being considered the definition of an intellectual.

The New York Times published two strongly critical obituaries. The print-based edition, *the more balanced of the two*, talked of,

> Chavez's dramatic sense of his own significance helped him to power as the reincarnation of the liberator Simon Bolivar – he even renamed the country.

Chavez's socialist legacy was, "the decay, dysfunction and blight that afflict the economy and every state institution" that the "bungling" Chavez had staffed with crooks and incompetents who "tried to impose pseudo-Marxism principles" (2013).

In reality, it was the Venezuelan people voted in 1999, by a factor of nearly three-to-one, to change the name of the country. And, as seen previously, the macro-economic indicators indicate an alternative interpretation, with GDP rising and unemployment and inflation falling.

But it was *The Miami Herald* who published the most negative obituary of all. Entitled "Venezuela's Hugo Chavez and his legacy of plunder", *The Herald* (2013a) described Chavez's "skilful rhetoric" that beguiled supporters with "utopian dreams" that was used to "methodologically destroy" Venezuela's democracy through rewriting the constitution, "rigging elections" and stifling adversaries. As a result, Venezuela became,

> A polarized society divided between the intolerant supporters of Mr. Chávez's Bolivarian Revolution and a democratic opposition that, against all odds, has waged a courageous fight for a democratic alternative.

The obituaries in the Western press differed little from opposition propaganda, *excepting that they were more critical*. *El Universal* (2013a), which led a coup to overthrow the government in 2002 (see Chapter 2), did note his "polarizing, sectarian and aggressive style with his adversaries" and the "openly Anti-American" current in the government, but did not question his sanity or call him a "dictator", "demagogue" or "despot" as the Western press did. Thus, the obituaries aligned themselves with the critical extreme of opinion on the subject, with no space reserved for positive portrayals. This venom was matched in statements made by many US officials, such as Ed Royce, Chairman of the House Foreign Affairs Committee expressed a similar opinion, and claimed:

> Hugo Chavez was a tyrant who forced the people of Venezuela to live in fear. His death dents the alliance of anti-US leftist leaders in South America. Good riddance to this dictator.
>
> (*Financial Times*, 2013)

Other analysis of Chavez's legacy

A testament to Hugo Chavez's impact on world politics was the level of interest around the world upon his passing. There were more than 800,000 tweets about Chavez on the day of his death, the large majority from outside Venezuela (*El Universal*, 2013b). The newspapers responded with a great number of news and commentary articles about his passing, his funeral and his legacy, the four British newspapers in the study publishing 69 separate articles in March alone. The more liberal newspapers in the study published *some* positive portrayals of the Venezuelan President. *The Guardian* published articles from the historian Tariq Ali and the feminist Selma James, who noted that Chavez was "the president of the poor who was loved by millions, especially by women, the poorest" (2013a). In *The Independent* (2013b) Owen Jones identified Chavez as a "democrat" who had greatly improved the lives of the poor. However, there were no positive articles whatsoever in the majority of newspapers.

In contrast, there was a great deal of negative portrayals of Chavez and his legacy in early 2013. *The Guardian* (2013b) likened European Chavez supporters to Maoist cult groups that threatened death on anyone who criticized the Chairman. Less than 24 hours after his passing, *The Daily Telegraph* published one article entitled "Hugo Chavez a Venezuelan Spartacus? A Latin American Kim Jong-Il, more like". On March 7th *The Times* (2013c) published a leading article entitled "The Perils of Populism" that stated, "literacy rates have changed little, income inequality has worsened and the poverty rate remains above 30 percent", all of which contradict the above data from the UN. Indeed, the UN's report shows that poverty fell more sharply in Venezuela in 2012 than in any other Latin American or Caribbean country (ECLAC, 2013: 15).

The Washington Post (2013a) described Chavez as, "A Marxist with a dash of Oprah" and stated, "he continues to have a near-mythical hold on the Venezuelan people. Even as the country crumbled around him, even as he leaves a legacy of ruin", and that he "produced a clone of Cuba's faltering communist state".

Thus, Hugo Chavez, a man who had won multiple clean elections, dramatically reduced inequality, poverty and extreme poverty, decreased unemployment and inflation, increased literacy rates, increased GNP per capita in Venezuela, a country where polls show that its citizens believe the country became substantially more democratic (see also Chapter 1), was presented in a less favourable light than King Abdullah, an absolute monarch boasting one of the worst human rights records in history. The key difference in this instance was that Abdullah was an ally of the British and American states and of neoliberal globalization that big business pushed for, whereas Chavez was its foe. The media ignored the reactions of the majority of the world leaders and the people of Venezuela, and continued to contradict the best empirical data available to side with their governments and business elites in condemning Chavez. Evidently, the dedication to state and business power is stronger than the custom of not speaking ill of the dead.

The funeral of Hugo Chavez

Thirty-three heads of state attended Chavez's funeral. This was in addition to delegations from more than 50 countries and international organizations. Of those 33 states, the CIA expresses no reservations about the quality of the democratic system of thirty of them, raising concerns only in the case of Cuba, Iran and Belarus (CIA, 2016), these countries often described by the US government as "outposts of tyranny" or as belonging to an "axis of evil". As noted in scholarship, the media have categorized the wave of the left-of-centre governments in Latin America as belonging to either a "good left" of responsible governments who accept the free market (Brazil, Chile, Uruguay) or a "bad left" of irresponsible repressive governments (Ecuador, Nicaragua, Bolivia, Venezuela, Argentina, Cuba) (Lupien, 2013; Young, 2013). The frequency with which countries with a head of state attending was counted. It is understandable that some small, geopolitically unimportant states such as St. Lucia may not be mentioned very often. Therefore, a control group was added: Mexico, a large, important state without a negative reputation.

In total, of the three "outposts of tyranny" Iran was mentioned 17 times, Cuba seven times and Belarus six times. Mexico, the control group with little to no negative image in the UK and US was not mentioned at all. The "good left" countries of Chile, Brazil and Uruguay were mentioned five times, while the "bad left" countries of Nicaragua, Bolivia, Ecuador, Cuba and Argentina were mentioned 29 times. All the other 22 attending countries put together were mentioned three times.

Table 3.3 Total number of 2013 mentions of heads of state attending Hugo Chavez's funeral

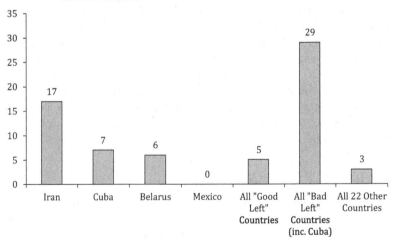

Therefore, the three states designated as "outposts of tyranny" were mentioned as many times as all other thirty democracies *combined*. Of those other countries, the large majority of those mentioned were the handful of "bad left" countries, who the media had also portrayed as repressive authoritarian regimes (Lupien, 2013; Young, 2013). Thus, the strong and false impression given was that Venezuela was a friend primarily of dictatorships and tyrannies. Indeed, this point was underscored in many of the articles. For example one *Washington Post* (2013b) article stated that Chavez was a special friend to other pariah states (emphasis added):

> "A great friend has died, a loyal friend, our brother," said Alexander Lukashenko, the president of Belarus, *a country the United States has called Europe's last dictatorship*. Another *friend* planning to attend is Iranian President Mahmoud Ahmadinejad.

The Daily Telegraph (2013c) did the same, noting that,

> A state funeral service attended by 33 heads of state, including Mahmoud Ahmadinejad, the Iranian president, and Alexander Lukashenko, the dictatorial president of Belarus, is still expected to go ahead today.

It was evidently insufficient simply to note that Castro, Ahmadinejad and Lukashenko attended; the newspapers underscored the assertion that they were dictators as well. The connection between Chavez and unsavoury characters did not end with heads of state. *The Independent* (2013c) informed its readers that a Russian gangster attended:

> Russia has sent the head of the state oil company Rosneft, Igor Sechin, an ally of Vladimir Putin who allegedly engineered the arrest of oligarch Mikhail Khodorkovsky and is described in the Moscow media as 'the scariest man on earth'.

Meanwhile, *The Times* (2013d) also alleged that Chavez had been training Hezbollah terrorists. It is perhaps understandable that the heads of state of smaller, less influential nations were not mentioned. Readers would not be expected to know these leaders. However, the large, influential nation of Mexico was not mentioned at all and Brazil, one of the largest and most important nations on the planet, was mentioned only once. This was despite it sending both its President,

Dilma Rousseff, and its ex-President, Lula, one of the world's most respected and well-known politicians.

Why *The Independent* mentioned the presence of Igor Sechin is unclear. Given the disparity with which various nations were mentioned, with the three nations dubbed "outposts of tyranny", or worse, in particular Iran, one strong hypothesis that could be drawn was that newspapers were attempting to portray Venezuela in a negative light by linking it with regimes associated with terror and repression. An alternative hypothesis that they were mentioned in great numbers because these were heads of state that readers would most be aware of fails, as states such as Brazil and Mexico, the control group were barely or never mentioned. Furthermore, as in the examples above, the newspapers often gave a short, negative biography to its readers of who President Lukashenko was.

Only weeks after Chavez's funeral, Venezuela was consumed by the presidential election between Chavez's successor Nicolas Maduro and Henrique Capriles Radonski. The following section deals with the election.

References

Anderson, J. L. (2013) "Slumlord: What Has Hugo Chavez Wrought in Venezuela?" *The New Yorker*, January 28th, www.newyorker.com/magazine/2013/01/28/slumlord

Buxton, J. (2013) "From Bust to Boom: Chavez's Economic Legacy," *Open Democracy*, March 7th, www.opendemocracy.net/opensecurity/julia-buxton/from-bust-to-boom-chavezs-economic-legacy

Cameron, D. (2015) "PM Statement on the Death of King Abdullah of Saudi Arabia," *Gov.uk*, January 23rd, www.gov.uk/government/news/pm-statement-on-the-death-of-king-abdullah-of-saudi-arabia

Carroll, R. (2013) *Comandante: The Life and Legacy of Hugo Chavez*, London: Cannongate.

CEPALSTAT (2016a) "Venezuela: National Socio-Demographic Profile," *CEPAL*, http://interwp.cepal.org/cepalstat/Perfil_Nacional_Social.html?pais=VEN&idioma=english

CEPALSTAT (2016b) "Millennium Development Goals: Country Profiles: Venezuela," *CEPAL*, http://interwp.cepal.org/perfil_ODM/perfil_Pais.asp?Pais=VEN&Id_idioma=2

CEPALSTAT (2016c) "Venezuela: National Economic Profile," *CEPAL*, http://interwp.cepal.org/cepalstat/Perfil_Nacional_Social.html?pais=VEN&idioma=english

CIA (2016) "The World Factbook," *CIA*, www.cia.gov/library/publications/the-world-factbook/

The Daily Telegraph (2013a) "Hugo Chavez," March 6th.

The Daily Telegraph (2013b) "Hugo Chavez, a Venezuelan Spartacus? A Latin American Kim Jong-Il More Like," March 6th.

The Daily Telegraph (2013c) "Hugo Chavez to Be Embalmed So 'His People Will Always Have Him,'" Match 8th.

The Daily Telegraph (2015) "King Abdullah Ibn Abdulaziz al-Saud," January 22nd.

Dangl, B. (2013) "What Chavez Left Behind: The Streets of a Continent and a Bolivarian Revolution of Everyday Life," *Upside Down World*, March 10th, http://upsidedownworld.org/main/venezuela-archives-35/4175-what-chavez-left-behind-the-streets-of-a-continent-and-a-bolivarian-revolution-of-everyday-life

Duno-Gottberg, L. (2013) "After Chavez: Re-Shifting the Focus," *Journal of Latin American Cultural Studies*, 22:2, pp. 239–241.

ECLAC (1990–2013) *Social Panorama of Latin America*, Santiago: United Nations.

El Universal (2013a) "La historia apenas comienza," March 6th, www.eluniversal.com/nacional-y-politica/hugo-chavez-1954-2013/130306/la-historia-apenas-comienza

El Universal (2013b) "Coberatura de la muerte de Chávez generó 804.434 tuits en el mundo," March 6th, www.eluniversal.com/nacional-y-politica/hugo-chavez-1954-2013/130306/cobertura-de-la-muerte-de-chavez-genero-804434-tuits-en-el-mundo#.UTm_eb9F9ps.twitter

El Universal (Colombia) (2013) "Evo Morales está 'destrozado' por la muerte de Chavez," March 5th, www.eluniversal.com.co/cartagena/actualidad/evo-morales-esta-destrozado-por-muerte-de-chavez-111104

FAO (2013) "Reconocimiento de la FAO a Venezuela," *FAO*, June 26th, www.fao.org/americas/noticias/ver/en/c/230150/

Ferguson, E. (2002) "Death Is the New Black," *The Guardian*, April 28th, www.theguardian.com/books/2002/apr/28/politics

Financial Times (2013) "Chavez as Divisive in Death as in Life," March 6th, www.ft.com/content/3e8db8b2-8631-11e2-ad73-00144feabdc0

The Guardian (2013a) "Hugo Chávez Knew That His Revolution Depended on Women," March 8th.

The Guardian (2013b) "Hugo Chavez: No Hero or Villain Please," March 6th.

Human Rights Watch (2013) "World Report: Saudi Arabia," www.hrw.org/world-report/2013/country-chapters/saudi-arabia

Humphrey, M. and Valverde, E. (2014) "Hope and Fear in Venezuelan Democracy: Violence, Citizen Insecurity, and Competing Neoliberal and Socialist Urban Imaginaries," in Angosto-Ferrandez, L. (ed.) *Democracy, Revolution and Geopolitics in Latin America: Venezuela and the International Politics of Discontent*, London: Routledge.

The Independent (2013a) "Hugo Chavez," March 7th.

The Independent (2013b) "In Death, This Democrat Will Be Called a Dictator," March 7th.

The Independent (2013c) "His Last Words: 'I Don't Want to Die,'" March 8th.

The Independent (2015) "King Abdullah of Saudi Arabia," January 25th.

Kozameh, S. (2013) "U.S. and Canada Isolated as Latin American Leaders Acknowledge Chavez's Regional Leadership," *CEPR*, March 6th, http://cepr.net/blogs/the-americas-blog/us-and-canada-isolated-as-latin-american-leaders-acknowledge-chavezs-regional-leadership

Lupien, P. (2013) "The Media in Venezuela and Bolivia: Attacking the 'Bad Left' From Below," *Latin American Perspectives*, 40, pp. 226–246.

Miami Herald (2013) "Venezuela's Hugo Chavez and His Legacy of Plunder," March 5th.

New York Times (2013) "In the End, an Awful Manager," March 6th.

New York Times (2015) "King Abdullah," January 22nd.

Obama, B. (2015) "Statement by the President on the Death of King Abdullah bin Abdulaziz," *The White House*, January 22nd, https://obamawhitehouse.archives.gov/the-press-office/2015/01/22/statement-president-death-king-abdullah-bin-abdulaziz

Plummer, R. (2013) "Hugo Chavez Leaves Venezuela in Economic Muddle," *BBC*, March 5th, www.bbc.co.uk/news/business-20795781

Sirota, D. (2013) "Hugo Chavez's Economic Miracle," *Salon*, March 6th, www.salon.com/2013/03/06/hugo_chavezs_economic_miracle/?socialism=love

TeleSur (2015) "In Their Own Words: Remembering Chavez," March 4th, www.telesurtv.net/english/analysis/In-Their-Own-Words-Remembering-Chavez-20150304-0016.html

The Times (2013a) "Hugo Chavez," March 6th.

The Times (2013b) "Last Hero of Hard Left Was Fidel With an Electoral Mandate . . . and a Christ Complex," March 6th.

The Times (2013c) "The Perils of Populism," March 7th.

The Times (2013d) "Loss of Its Leading Man Spells the End for the Opaque Axis of Diesel," March 7th.

Times Live (2013) "Zuma Sends Condolences to Venezuela," March 6th, www.timeslive.co.za/politics/2013/03/06/zuma-sends-condolences-to-venezuela

Toro, F. (2013) "Chavez Wasn't Just a Zany Buffoon, He Was an Oppressive Autocrat," *The Atlantic*, March 5th, www.theatlantic.com/international/archive/2013/03/chavez-wasnt-just-a-zany-buffoon-he-was-an-oppressive-autocrat/273745/

UNDP (2010) *Cumpliendo las Metas del Milenio*, www.undp.org/content/dam/undp/library/MDG/english/MDG%20Country%20Reports/Venezuela/Venezuela_MDGReport_2010_SP.pdf

UNDP (2013) *Venezuela: HDI Values and Rank Changes in the 2013 Human Development Report*, http://hdr.undp.org/sites/default/files/Country-Profiles/VEN.pdf

UNDP (2015) *Human Development Report*, http://report.hdr.undp.org/

Unite (2013) "Unite Stands Shoulder to Shoulder With Venezuela Following Chavez's Death," *Unite*, March 6th, www.unitetheunion.org/news/unitestandsshouldertoshoulderwithvenezuelafollowingchavezsdeath/

Washington Post (2013a) "A Marxist With a Dash of Oprah," March 10th.

Washington Post (2013b) "Taking up Chavez's Torch," March 9th.

Weisbrot, M. and Sandoval, L. (2007) "The Venezuelan Economy in the Chavez Years," *CEPR*, www.cepr.net/index.php/publications/reports/the-venezuelan-economy-in-the-chavez-years

Weyland, K. (2013) "Why Latin America Is Becoming Less Democratic," *The Atlantic*, July 15th, www.theatlantic.com/international/archive/2013/07/why-latin-america-is-becoming-less-democratic/277803/

World Bank (2016) "Venezuela, RB," http://data.worldbank.org/country/venezuela-rb

Young, K. (2013) "The Good, the Bad, and the Benevolent Interventionist: U.S. Press and Intellectual Distortions of the Latin American Left," *Latin American Perspectives*, 40:3 (May), pp. 207–225.

4 The 2013 elections

Following Chavez's death, his Vice-President, Nicolas Maduro narrowly beat challenger Henrique Capriles in controversial April presidential elections.

Competing narratives on the elections

The opposition frame

The Venezuelan opposition generally accepted that the electoral process in Venezuela is clean. Vicente Díaz, senior opposition member of the Venezuelan Electoral Council (CNE) said he had "no doubts" about the veracity of the election results (*The Miami Herald*, 2013f). However, it charged that the CNE is biased and the government uses state resources to tip the balance of power in its favour by funding its election campaigns, using the state's vast array of media networks to pump out propaganda (*The Real News*, 2012), and that it pressures hundreds of thousands of state employees to vote for the *chavistas* (*The Miami Herald*, 2013a).

This opinion is put forward by those at the critical end of the academic spectrum, such as Naím (2014), who claims that the government uses an array of "dirty tricks" such as buying votes and shutting down critical television channels, and Corrales and Penfold (2011: 1), who state that "die-hard loyalists of the government are placed at top-level positions in state offices, such as the courts, thereby undermining the system of checks and balances".

The Chavista frame

In contrast, the Venezuelan government highlights the technical achievements of the electoral system and its transparency and sophistication. The government categorize the elections as free and fair and "a model for the region" to follow (Embassy of Venezuela, 2012). It notes that Venezuelan elections are among the most carefully monitored in the world by election-monitoring bodies and outside observers, who attest to the robustness of the system, its openness and its transparency (Ibid). In total contrast to the opposition narrative, the *chavistas* claim the opposition has a great advantage in the election process, as the vast majority of media networks are in private hands and are highly critical of the government, even fomenting a coup in 2002, and that the opposition is funded and supported by Washington. Therefore, the media are active participants in protecting the country from further democratization (Kitzberger, 2012).

Academics sympathetic to the government highlight the great number of elections in Venezuela that Chavez won. Bhatt (2013) notes Chavez won some 14 in 13 years, which he characterizes as "free and fair". Carasik (2015) argues that the election system is unfairly maligned, characterizing it as "one of the most efficient, secure and transparent electoral systems" in the world.

These two interpretations of Venezuelan elections starkly contrast. There was a similarly wide reaction to the results of the elections and Capriles' protestations.

International reactions to the elections

The Union of South American Nations (UNASUR) came out strongly in favour of Maduro and the elections. On April 19th it congratulated the Venezuelan people and recognized Maduro as the rightful President. Furthermore, it urged Capriles to respect the results and the CNE and demanded that the violent protests desist (UNASUR, 2013). A great number of other countries, such as Mexico, Canada and Russia quickly recognized Maduro, thereby shunning Capriles.

In contrast, the United States did not recognize Maduro's victory, with White House spokesperson Jay Carney (2013) standing with Capriles in his calls for a 100 percent audit, declaring it a prudent and necessary step. Spain also initially took this position. However, seeing that much of the rest of the world had backed Maduro and the legitimacy of the elections, and after the lethal protests/riots flared up, it reversed its position, siding with UNASUR. It issued a statement calling on "all political actors" – i.e. Capriles, to respect the CNE's results and formally recognizing Maduro as the legitimate President-Elect (Gobierno de España, 2013), and claiming it had never held the previous position. Thus, by April 19th, the US was isolated in its support of Capriles and its questioning of the results.

Although Capriles himself is a major actor in Venezuelan politics, there is no agreement on what or whom he represents. Capriles presents himself as a reformer, a moderate, and an admirer of the former Brazilian President Lula, a socialist from the Workers' Party. *NBC* presented Capriles as a youthful, "center-left progressive" whose "inclusive approach" has proved very popular with ordinary Venezuelans (NBC, 2012).

In contrast, the noted Venezuelan playwright and intellectual Luis Britto García characterizes Capriles as a "fascist creep" and an "ultra-super-reactionary" who rose to prominence after cutting his teeth in a "fanatical fascist group, somewhere between a religious and a political organization" (Lovato, 2014). The organization, Tradition, Family and Property, was banned in 1984 after it tried to assassinate the Pope. The opinion that Capriles is a fascist is common among those sympathetic to the government; one foreign Ambassador in Caracas describing him as "the face of fascism" as Capriles' mob attacked his embassy in 2002 during the coup (Sanchez, 2007: 141–160).

In between these two extremes, one can find a full range of viewpoints on Capriles considering him as moderate, conservative or far right. Carroll (2013: 278), for instance, presents Capriles as a glamorous, charismatic and capable moderate while Tinker-Salas (2015: 204) characterizes him as a conservative. Evidence of his character and motivations beyond other people's opinions is presented later.

Empirical evidence

The Venezuelan voting system has drawn praise from all over the world (Carter Center: 2013, European Parliament, 2005, European Union Election Observation Mission, 2006). In order to vote, Venezuelans must have their ID card and their fingerprint scanned. If these matches are successful, they vote electronically and check then place their paper receipt into a ballot box. The vote is counted automatically but a random audit of 53 percent is counted manually.[1] Each station's paper and electronic vote must match perfectly, and the process is watched over all day by representatives of all parties and by international observers in what are some of the most monitored elections in the world. The overly secure system was brought in in 1998 and significantly improved later in reaction to the very low public confidence in the veracity of elections. During the October 2012 elections, the audit of the machines found 22 total cases of discrepancy between electronic and paper tally as 22 Venezuelans failed to put their paper ballot in the box after voting electronically (Carter Center, 2013: 20).

There have been a great number of reports from international organizations monitoring the Venezuelan elections. The Carter Center, a Washington-based election monitoring organization funded primarily by multinational corporations and the US Government, headed by former US President Jimmy Carter and anti-Chavez academic Jennifer McCoy, observed the 1998 Presidential elections where they "found no significant problems", in "one of the most transparent elections in the country's history" (Trinkunas and McCoy, 1998: 14).

The European Union's reports on the 2005 and 2006 elections lauded the electoral system. In 2005 it noted,

> The security and transparency measures introduced in the automated voting process are in line with the most advanced international practice.(European Parliament, 2005: 15)

Whereas in 2006 it claimed:

> The electronic voting system established in Venezuela is efficient, secure and auditable, and the competence of the technical experts is in line with its advanced technological level.
> (European Union Election Observation Mission, 2006: 4)

It also commented upon the media, noting that there was a "great diversity of political opinions" offered, although noting its highly partisan nature (European Parliament, 2005: 15).

Positive reports from election observers have continued since then. Indeed, President Carter (2012) stated in 2012 that "I would say the election process in Venezuela is the best in the world . . . they have a very wonderful voting system".

The polling company Latinobarómetro found that in 1997, 83 percent of Venezuelans believed elections to be fraudulent and 11 percent to be clean. However, by 2006, only 30 percent believed them to be fraudulent, with 56 percent believing them to be clean. The survey data also showed that Venezuelans had a very high opinion of their democracy. Indeed, when compared with the other countries of Latin America, Venezuela fared extremely well.

The CNE declared Nicolas Maduro to be the winner of the elections, by a count of 51 to 49 percent. A random sample of 53 percent of the ballots was manually checked against the electronic vote, finding no discrepancies. The Carter Center (2013: 67) noted that both Maduro and Capriles' parties provided witnesses for around 91 percent of polling stations.

Capriles, going against what his own party's elections expert stated, refused to accept the result, claiming fraud, and demanded an audit of 100 percent of the ballots cast. He called his supporters onto the

Table 4.1 How democratic is your country? 2013, average score, Latino-barómetro

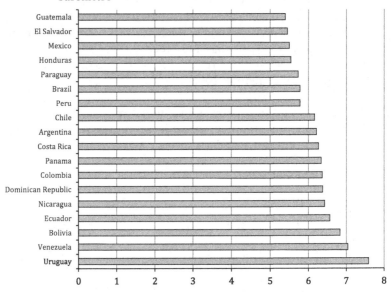

streets to demonstrate. Health clinics and the doctors inside them were attacked. The Carter Center counted at least eight people killed and 78 injured during the demonstrations (Ibid: 16). Some observers derided Capriles' rejection of the results and his and Washington's demands for a 100 percent audit. For instance, economist David Rosnick calculated that the probability of the audit overturning the result was "far less than one in 25,000,000,000,000,000" or one in 25 thousand trillion (Rosnick and Weisbrot, 2007). Nevertheless, on April 18th, the CNE agreed to a 100 percent audit of the vote, although its president made it clear that she agreed to Capriles' demands only to prevent further bloodshed on the streets (Carter Center, 2013: 21).

But on April 22nd, Capriles rejected the CNE's acquiescence and came up with a new set of demands which entailed checking all 15 million thumbprints and signatures individually. The CNE explained that his request was unconstitutional and beyond its remit. Under Venezuelan law the legal vote is the electronic vote, and the paper tally is effectively a receipt of voting. It also noted that the 100 percent audit was a *de facto* recount anyway. Furthermore, voters' anonymity would have been compromised if the recount had taken place (Ibid: 26–27).

Capriles boycotted the audit he had requested the previous week. The audit found the original result was accurate to a degree of 99.98 percent. While one explanation for this is a misunderstanding or miscommunication, another explanation for the affair is that Capriles was moving the goalposts in order to allow his allies in the international media to use their cultural power to frame the event as fraud. It should be noted that this was a common action from the opposition, who refused to recognize any *chavista* victories until 2006. One example was in 2004, where the opposition lost 41 to 59 percent. They claimed it was fraudulent and took to the streets. However, no formal complaints were lodged with the CNE. When the Bush administration endorsed the results, one newspaper wrote, "Bush has abandoned us" (Dominguez, 2011: 124).

While generally praising the 2013 election, the Carter Center's report did highlight some shortfalls. For instance, it cited a number of Venezuelan civil society organizations that claimed that at a minority of polling stations both opposition and *chavistas* had used government vehicles to transport people to vote (2013: 68), while a small number of people (less than one percent) reported feeling pressured when voting, both sides being guilty of this (Ibid: 68). Electoral propaganda was visible inside the 200-metre legal limit at some voting stations while there were Maduro campaign posters in many government buildings. The Carter Center criticized Dr. Lucena for wearing a black armband associated with Chavez at the President's funeral and for accepting Maduro's request that, for security reasons, he should be allowed to vote in Caracas rather than in his home state, Carabobo. The report noted these could be examples of bias and favouritism (Ibid: 45). Furthermore, the majority of top CNE officials were Chavez supporters or sympathizers.

It should be noted, however, that the Carter Center has its own biases. It is funded by Washington and headed by an academic who does not hide her criticisms of Chavez and Maduro. Its Programme Director, Jennifer McCoy, claimed that Chavez displayed "autocratic instincts as strong of those" as Pedro Carmona, a week after he had kidnapped Chavez and abolished the Supreme Court, the National Assembly and the CNE (*The New York Times*, 2002) (see Chapter Two). One example of bias in the report is it spent a great deal of time scrutinizing the transgressions of the government but did not mention the well-documented US government funding, training and support of opposition groups (Beeton et al., 2015: 518). Given the biases it displays, the results from the Carter Center are particularly notable.

The next section will explore the empirical data with regard to the Venezuelan media and elections.

The media

Television is the dominant and most important media in Venezuela, penetrating 92.2 percent of households (Carter Center, 2013: 47). The polling company AGB Nielsen monitored Venezuelan television market share throughout the 2000's. Private television stations such as Gustavo Cisneros' *Venevisión* dominate the airwaves. In comparison, Venezuelan state television accounts for a very small percentage of viewership (5 percent in 2010). The data in the following graph is taken from the January figure for each year.

The state's share of the market expanded from 2 percent in 2000 to 5 percent in 2010 and 5.4 percent by late 2012 (BBC, 2012). However, this remained marginal in comparison with private and paid television.

Pay television, analogous to cable or satellite television in the US and UK, is very popular. In 2007, the influential terrestrial TV channel *RCTV* did not have its license renewed, so it moved to pay television, hence the rise in pay TV and drop in private. Nearly all pay TV is private, with the exception of *Asamblea*, a state-owned pay TV channel with limited viewership. AGB Nielsen did not distinguish between public and private pay TV channels, otherwise the numbers would have been more pronounced.

Table 4.2 Venezuelan TV audience share, 2000–2010, AGB Nielsen, cited in Weisbrot and Ruttenburg (2010: 2–4)

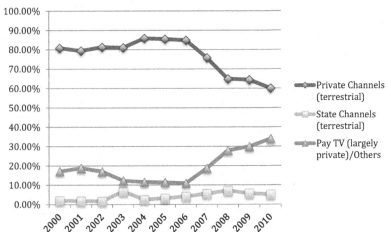

For radio, it is a similar picture. Seventy percent of Venezuela's radio and TV stations are privately owned, with slightly less than 5 percent in state hands with private, commercial outlets dominating the airwaves (BBC, 2012). In terms of print media, four major papers, *El Nacional, El Universal, Meridiano* and *Últimas Noticias* control 86 percent of the circulation (Lupien, 2013). The first three maintain anti-government positions while the fourth is categorized as pro-government.

The Carter Center also monitored television media throughout the April elections. One of its findings echoed previous election monitoring missions that television media in the country is deeply partisan, with state television backing the *chavistas* and private media backing the opposition. Private television concentrated on Capriles' campaign, devoting 73 percent of its coverage to the challenger, while state TV's bias was even more pronounced, devoting 90 percent of its coverage to Maduro (Carter Center, 2013: 56). As shown here, the private stations displayed a strong tendency to portray Henrique Capriles positively

Table 4.3 Venezuelan media assessment of Maduro and Capriles, Carter Center (2013: 56)

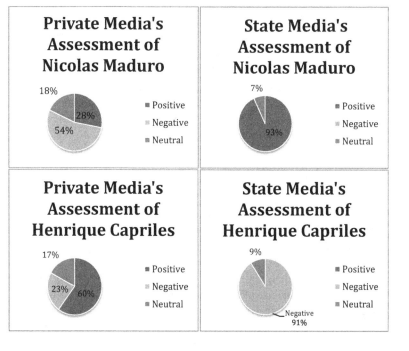

and Nicolas Maduro negatively while state TV overwhelmingly portrayed Capriles negatively and Maduro positively.

However, an AGB Nielsen study showed that *VTV*, the main state-TV channel obtained a comparatively small 8.4 percent of the Venezuelan television market between January and June 2013, trailing Cisneros' *Venevisión*, which obtained 22.9 percent (Carter Center, 2013: 47).

The CNE conducted its own study of the coverage, and, thanks to the disparity in reach between private and public stations, found *that Capriles received nearly double the coverage of Maduro on the six main terrestrial TV channels in the run up to the election* (Ibid: 49–50). It also studied the prevalence of campaign ads by each camp on television. While state television often exceeded the legal limit of 240 seconds per day for either candidate, *Televen*, Cisneros' *Venevisión* and in particular *Globovisión* broadcasted up to two and a half times the maximum legal time limit for the opposition every day in the April running up to the election (Ibid: 51).

The data show that large, private channels critical of the government dominate Venezuela. The Venezuelan state's television market share is markedly small, not only in comparison with private channels, but also with many other countries with public broadcasters. For instance, government-owned TV accounted for 37 percent of market share in France and 38 percent in the UK over the same period (Weisbrot and Ruttenberg, 2010: 6). While the smaller state television barely allows pro-opposition content, the larger, private media display a strong bias against the government and in favour of the opposition. The data *strongly* challenge the opposition narrative of a government dominating the airwaves. In fact, Capriles received far more television coverage, the majority of it positive, than Maduro, whose coverage in the media was mostly negative anyway. The next section deals with opposition leader, Henrique Capriles.

Henrique Capriles Radonski

As shown above, Henrique Capriles has been interpreted as everything from a socialist progressive to a conservative to a neo-fascist. Capriles presents himself as a progressive social-democrat whose political inspiration is Lula da Silva, the socialist former President of Brazil (Padgett, 2012). It must be stated, however, that Lula himself has rejected Capriles, claiming it "absurd" that he would support him (*Correo del Orinoco*, 2012) and publicly endorsed Maduro and actively campaigned against Capriles in 2012.

Capriles portrays himself as coming from humble origins, his Jewish grandparents having fled Europe during World War Two. However, he is also a product of two of the richest and most influential families in Venezuela: the Caprileses and the Radonskis. His mother is the owner of the largest chain of private movie theatres in Venezuela while his father is a food magnate responsible for establishing the giant Kraft Foods in Venezuela. The Capriles family also owns *Cadena Capriles*, one of Venezuela's largest and most powerful media empires, which included the influential *Últimas Noticias* newspaper (until October, 2013) and many best-selling magazines. He became a lawyer and studied at an Ivy League university. Capriles has generally represented the right wing of the opposition, having been a member of COPEI, the more conservative of Venezuela's two main elitist parties in the *Punto Fijo* period (1958–98). Capriles was also a prominent member of a mob who attacked the Cuban embassy during the 2002 coup and then publicly arrested/kidnapped the *chavista* Interior Minister on live television.

For those wishing to gauge Capriles' political position, it would be useful to read his 1200 policy proposal promises for the October 2012 election, the *Lineamientos*. The *Lineamientos* advocate a swift return to neoliberalism with a strong emphasis on wide-scale privatization and/or business influence, for instance in the Central Bank (407–9), the electricity supply (424), the oil industry (497), the healthcare service (882) and schools (822). It proposes a return to free trade (1232) and closely working with the World Bank and IMF again (403) along with a great rise in the price of water (1001). They also highlight the opposition's commitment to "private property, economic freedom and private initiative" (43). They also plan to redesign national curriculums at all levels in order to teach children "the connection between property, economic progress, political liberty and social development" (612) (MUD, 2012; Cannon, 2014). Thus, Capriles' proposals effectively advocate a course of economic and social "shock therapy", not dissimilar to those carried out by the IMF, World Bank and University of Chicago in Latin American countries such as Chile in 1973.

Analysis

The elections of 2013: clean or unclean?

Of the 197 articles in the 2013 sample, the UK newspapers identified Venezuelan elections as clean 16 times and unclean 48 times. The US newspapers identified them as clean six times and unclean 76 times.

Table 4.4 Venezuelan elections: clean or not clean? 2013 newspaper identifications

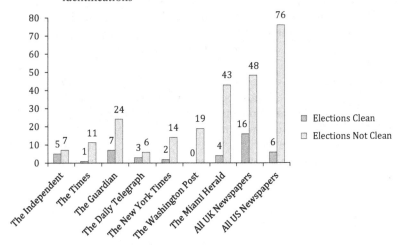

While the British newspapers showed a pronounced tendency towards describing elections as unclean (a 3:1 ratio), it produced more equal coverage that the US, where there was an overwhelming tendency to describe the elections as unfair or unclean. Of course, some of the coverage revolved around Henrique Capriles crying fraud, which would increase the number of "not clean" presentations. However, it is journalistic custom to counter an accusation with the opposing point of view from the other side, which, in this case included government officials, the CNE, election observers and the great majority of foreign governments. The results show that this was not done frequently. Indeed, many of the identifications of clean Venezuelan elections came in opinion pieces following Hugo Chavez's death. Identifications of fair elections were less common in the American newspapers.

Even when the electronic voting was not attacked, the veracity of the election results were undermined, *The Daily Telegraph* (2013a) quoted one observer stating,

> 'I trust the machines, it's the humans I worry about,' added Mr Marrero, 'If Capriles wins we can expect violence. The Chavistas don't know how to lose.'

This statement is notable in that the opposition has often turned to violence following electoral defeat, and the day after this story was published Capriles supporters demonstrated and eleven people were killed. In contrast, *chavistas* have always accepted their election defeats peacefully.

There was around five times as much space devoted to the possibility of unclean elections as there was to the idea of clean elections. Sometimes the credibility of the CNE and the believability of the audit were called into question but it was more common to attack the credibility of the elections on the idea that the *chavistas* had "slanted the playing field" (*The Miami Herald*, 2013a) by coercing voters to the polls, buying votes or using state funds to bankroll their campaigns, exactly the line the opposition themselves took, as shown previously. In British newspapers this idea was generally raised as a (believable) accusation, whereas in the American media it was presented as a fact that the *chavistas* had a clearly unfair advantage. For instance, *The Daily Telegraph* (2013b) reported about the "litany of complaints" against the government, Capriles accusing it of,

> Shamelessly abusing its power in order to ensure the election former president Hugo Chavez's designated heir. He accused Mr. Maduro of 'abusing power, abusing state resources' by appearing on television lavishing praise on the late president over the weekend, even though officially campaigning should have stopped.

Meanwhile, *The New York Times* (2013a) presented the slanted playing field idea as a fact, claiming that the government has an overwhelming "get-out-the-vote machine" that taps "nearly unlimited" public resources and that government workers are required to attend its rallies, concluding,

> Most observers say the field is tilted strongly in Mr. Maduro's favor, citing a court system packed with loyalists and an electoral council that refuses to curb the use of government resources in the campaign.

The conservative American newspapers had still stronger opinions than *The New York Times*. In an editorial, *The Washington Post* (2013a) claimed that,

> Unsurprisingly, polls show that Mr. Maduro will win this grossly one-sided contest. If by some chance he does not, the regime is unlikely to accept the results.

Thus, the newspapers' supposedly balanced reporting closely mirrored the opposition's official line and went against professional American election observers' pronouncements. Indeed, many editorials were far more critical of the elections than the opposition themselves, who rated their democratic system an average 5/10 in a Latinobarómetro survey that year.

On the subject of election monitors' and international organizations' praise for the quality and veracity of the elections, which contrasted greatly with way the newspaper covered the events, *The Miami Herald* (2013b) claimed,

> Other groups such as UNASUR explicitly exclude the United States and Canada and have neither the competency nor arguably the inclination to review Venezuela's election results objectively.

Thus, pronouncing the organizations incompetent solved the problem of contrary opinions of the elections. The problem of American isolation on the issue of recognition of the elections was solved largely by ignoring its existence.

The Miami Herald (2013a) also reported claims that "during the last two votes there was also evidence that the country's 2.4 million public-sector workers, and hundreds of thousands of government welfare recipients, were being pressured to vote along party lines". This contradicts the US government-funded Carter Center (2013: 68), who found that very few people reported being pressured into voting (under one percent), but, in fact, *twice as many people reported feeling pressured into voting for Capriles than for Maduro.*

It was, however, on the question of the Venezuelan media that the newspapers focussed upon most.

The Venezuelan media

This study monitored the frequency of four positions asserted by the media: whether the Venezuelan media was free or caged, and whether state media does or does not dominate the airwaves. The "caged" frame represented any time a story implied or stated that the Venezuelan media were coerced or cowed by the government. The state dominating the media narrative included any time an article noted that the Venezuelan state had a wide array of media outlets or implied that it dominated the market. Counted in the opposite frame was any time an article mentioned that the private sector in fact dominated market-share in any category of media or simply that the government did not dominate the market.

The sample was recorded across the years 1998–2014. However, it was the 2013 sample that discussed the media much more often. UK newspapers claimed that the Venezuelan media was caged 56 times (18 times is 2013) but did not claim they were free at all. It implied or stated state-media dominated the market 13 times (seven in 2013) and implied or stated it did not 3 times (once in 2013).

Over the same time period, US newspapers identified the Venezuelan media was caged 110 times (36 times in 2013 alone) but never once as free. It implied that government-owned media dominated the market 26 times (14 times in 2013) and implied or stated the opposite once (and never in 2013). The following quotes are all from the 2013 sample period.

Similar to other issues, the data show that all newspapers largely took positions at the far end of the critical spectrum of expressed opinions about Venezuela. It also showed that conservative newspapers took a more critical stance than liberal ones and American newspapers were more critical than British ones.

The Daily Telegraph (2013c) noted:

> Opinions polls suggest that the residual sentiment from Chavez's death, and the huge advantages that Chavez built into the system during his years in power, controlling the media and some four million government jobs, will be enough to carry Mr Maduro to victory.

Table 4.5 Venezuelan media: caged or free? 1998–2014

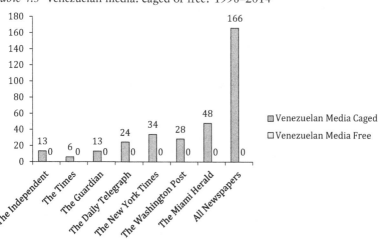

Table 4.6 The Venezuelan state: does it dominate the media landscape or not?

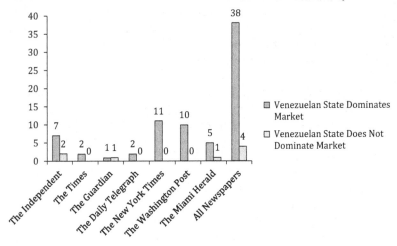

The *Independent* (2013a) claimed Maduro had a huge advantage, including the backing of a state media "empire" in a country where "there is now just one private TV station" critical of the government, meaning that the dynamic and energetic Capriles had to travel across the country to "outflank" the all-powerful "dominance" of the government's media empire.

Thus, the British press presented the elections as a David vs. Goliath battle, where the underdog Capriles mounted a "grassroots" challenge against a grossly unfair playing field where Maduro's overwhelming state-media complex bombarded Venezuelans with propaganda and handed out jobs in return for votes. Capriles was presented as unable to get his voice heard in the media. This is in total contrast to the empirical studies, and in reality the Capriles family owned one of the largest media empires in Latin America.

The American press presented the situation in a similar manner. *The Miami Herald* (2013c) stated, as a matter of fact:

> The media disparity is one of the most visible example of the government's campaign advantage. While a bevy of state-run media openly back Maduro, Capriles has to compete for time on cowed private media, said Carlos Correa, with the Espacio Público media watchdog group.

Empirical data published by sources unfriendly toward the *chavistas* showed that, not only do private media dominate the airwaves, but also that they came out strongly in support of Capriles. As noted previously, Capriles "competed" on the "cowed" private media by receiving three times as much coverage as Maduro on the four private terrestrial channels, who portrayed Capriles positively 60 percent of the time and negatively 23 percent. In contrast, they presented Maduro positively 28 percent and negatively 54 percent of the time. All four of the private terrestrial channels ran more Capriles ads than Maduro ads, three of whom devoted so much attention to Capriles that *every day of the campaign period they broke the law that imposes a legal maximum limit*. Furthermore, the empirical studies did not include the dozens of private non-terrestrial TV channels. In contrast to *The Independent's* (2013a) assertion that "there is just one private TV station critical of 'Chavismo' ", a notion reproduced in *The Washington Post* (2013b), who asserted that "Venezuela's all-powerful government" was about to shut it down or co-opt *Globovisión*, the data show that *every private Venezuelan station in the sample displayed a strong anti-government and pro-opposition bias*. Far from state-owned media dominating the market, in reality state-owned media had a very small percentage of audience share, both in comparison with private media and in comparison with the UK and other Western countries.

As to the existence of any opinions straying from the narrative the media presented, *The Guardian* (2013) categorically stated that there was none (emphasis added):

> *It is not disputed* that, under Chavez, political posts were stuffed with his supporters, judicial processes gerrymandered, judges cowed, and critical media sanctioned whenever its toe strayed across a highly diaphanous line.

Diaphanous, meaning delicate, weak and thin, suggests that any criticism of the government was intolerable and punished. Therefore, any mention of alternative opinions on the subject, of which there are very many (Lupien, 2013; Fernandes, 2010; Duno-Gottberg, 2009, 2011), was rendered unnecessary by stating factually that these opinions did not exist.

The empirical data strongly suggests a different conclusion to the question of the liberty and biases of the Venezuelan media during this period. The newspapers unwaveringly presented the media as caged, cowed and not free to say what they wanted. They also presented the state-run media as dominating the airwaves, an assertion proven incorrect. In short, the Western media consistently contradicted the best empirical evidence available in order to side with the positions of their governments and corporations at the critical extreme of the spectrum. The empirical data used was taken from well-known reputable sources unsympathetic to the government of Venezuela, easily available online in English. It would, in other words, be the *first place* a journalist might turn to for quotable and dependable statistics about the media. During an interview for this book, Pascal Lupien said:

> I have a hard time understanding how anyone can argue that there is no critical TV media left in Venezuela because it is so clearly not true. One can simply watch television for five minutes or read any of the newspapers to debunk that myth.

A statement that begs the question: what have journalists covering Venezuela been doing?

The above quotes about the media presented Henrique Capriles as an underdog mounting a grassroots, bottom up campaign that inspired millions of Venezuelans who want change. The final section deals with him in more detail.

Henrique Capriles Radonski

In total, Capriles was identified positively 45 times and negatively six times. His involvement in a coup was mentioned twice, although on both occasions his guilt was unclear. Indeed, *The Miami Herald's* (2013c) allusion to it presented it as an accusation, that charges against him had been dropped, his counter that he had been "defraying tensions" and a quote from him saying, "I am a democrat."

The quantitative analysis suggests there was a very strong tendency to portray Capriles positively. However, qualitative analysis shows that the presentation of Capriles was much *more* positive than the quantitative analysis suggests. All six of the negative identifications came from senior *chavista* politicians literally cursing at him. Five articles mentioned a politician calling him a "fascist" while the sixth mentioned that Maduro "scoffed" at him, calling him a "little prince of the parasitical bourgeoisie" (*The Times*, 2013a). All negative identifications of Capriles came in the form of insults levelled at him by politicians the newspapers had been defaming for years and in contexts trying to illustrate the supposed intolerance and bitterness of the *chavistas* and therefore were of a very low weight. Thus, he was presented virtually unanimously positively.

In contrast, the positive descriptions of Capriles were presented as statements of fact, not opinions or hearsay. When described, Capriles was consistently portrayed as a youthful (eight articles), charismatic

Table 4.7 2013 Newspapers' identifications of Henrique Capriles

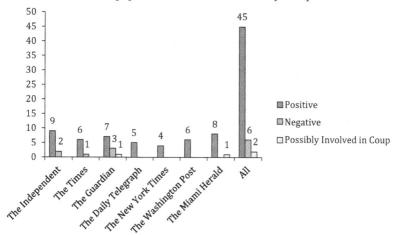

(three articles), energetic (six articles), underdog with great organizing skills campaigning against a mighty government apparatus. Indeed, in the October 2012 Presidential elections against an ailing Chavez, *The Financial Times* (2012) characterized the contest as a "David and Goliath contest". Given the Capriles' wealthy upbringing, his family's ownership of one of the largest media empires in South America, the Venezuelan media's bias against the government, the opposition's corporate backing and the US government's generous funding of his political activities, the analogy may prove inexact. A typical description of Capriles came from *The Independent* (2013a), that wrote:

> As the energetic governor of the state of Miranda, Mr Capriles campaigned across the country, building support from the grassroots upwards in the face of Mr Chavez's dominance of state media.

Capriles' political position was frequently discussed in the articles. *The Times* (2013a) noted:

> Henrique Capriles, the progressive governor of Miranda state . . . 40, a baseball-loving bachelor who models his economic and social manifesto on that of the leftist Brazil, will have sought the presidency.

This quote is illustrative of many articles that presented Capriles as a progressive and a Lula disciple, despite the fact that Lula had very publicly rejected Capriles and endorsed Chavez and Maduro.

The Miami Herald also presented Capriles as a left-winger, noting that he was "running as a center-left reformer who wants to weed out corruption and cronyism but has also vowed to protect the poor and needy" (2014d) and claiming that "*chavistas* abandoned Maduro in droves as Capriles' center-left platform and calls for political reconciliation struck a chord" (2014e).

Other newspapers presented Capriles as a moderate. *The Independent* (2013a) identified him as "the centrist governor of Miranda state" while one *Times* (2013b) article did the same, calling him "the centrist state governor". Serious identifications of Capriles representing the right-wing were absent; the closest was *The New York Times* (2013b) noting that he managed to "inject hope" into the opposition and build "a coalition of groups from across the political spectrum".

The idea of Henrique Capriles representing a centrist, a social-democratic or a progressive was presented as factual information whereas any idea of him representing the right wing was mentioned only as an insult in the mouths of individuals the newspapers had been criticizing for years. This is particularly noteworthy as Capriles' background, the political groups he was part of, his actions and his 1,200 policy proposals all support the right-wing thesis.

To conclude, all newspapers sampled, with some variation in tone and presentation, portrayed the 2013 presidential elections as, at best, hotly disputed and at worst a "grossly one-sided" sham presided over by a dictatorship. This went against the opinion of every country in the world except the United States, and against a Nobel Prize-winning American election-monitoring organization the US government had paid to observe it. The media unanimously presented the Venezuelan media as caged, not free, and dominated by the state, going against the best empirical studies. In short, the media presented minority opinions on highly contentious issues as incontrovertible facts, often not even acknowledging or even denying the majority opinion's existence, despite empirical data overwhelmingly supporting the majority's view. When it was mentioned, it was usually presented in the form of an accusation made by a source of little validity.

Note

1 During the 2016 Presidential election, states were being called for Clinton or Trump after 0.1 percent of the votes were counted.

References

BBC (2012) "In Depth: Media in Venezuela," *BBC*, October 3rd, www.bbc.co.uk/news/world-latin-america-19368807

Beeton, D., Johnston, J. and Main, A. (2015) "'Venezuela," in Wikileaks (ed.) *Wikileaks: The World According to the US Empire*, London:
Verso.

Bhatt, K. (2013) "The Hypocrisy of Human Rights Watch," *NACLA Report
on the Americas*, 46:4, p. 55.

Cannon, B. (2014) "As Clear as MUD: Characteristics, Objectives, and Strat-
egies of the Opposition in Bolivarian Venezuela," *Latin American Politics
and Society*, 56:4, pp. 49–70.

Carasik, L. (2015) "Venezuela's Electoral System Is Being Unfairly Maligned,"
Al-Jazeera, November 30th, http://america.aljazeera.com/opinions/2015/11/
venezuelas-electoral-system-is-being-unfairly-maligned.html

Carney, J. (2013) "Press Briefing by Press Secretary Jay Carney," *The White
House*, April 15th, www.whitehouse.gov/the-press-office/2013/04/15/press-
briefing-press-secretary-jay-carney-4152013

Carroll, R. (2013) *Comandante: The Life and Legacy of Hugo Chavez*, London: Cannongate.

Carter, J. (2012) "30 Years of the Cater Center," September 21st, www.youtube.
com/watch?v=VPKPw4t6Sic#t=43m33

The Carter Center (2013) "Preliminary Report Study Mission of the Carter
Center: Presidential Elections in Venezuela, April 14, 2013," www.cartercenter.
org/resources/pdfs/news/peace_publications/election_reports/venezuela-
pre-election-rpt-2013.pdf

Ciccariello-Maher, G. (2016) *Building the Commune: Radical Democracy in
Venezuela*, London: Verso.

Corrales, J. and Penfold, M. (2011) *Dragon in the Tropics: Hugo Chavez and
the Political Economy of Revolution in Venezuela*, Washington, DC: Brookings Institution.

Correo del Orinoco (2012) "Lula Da Silva respalda reelección del president
Hugo Chávez," March 22nd, www.correodelorinoco.gob.ve/nacionales/lula-
da-silva-respalda-reeleccion-presidente-hugo-chavez/

The Daily Telegraph (2013a) "Venezuela Election: Capriles Accuses Socialists
of Abusing Power to Ensure Maduro Win," April 14th.

The Daily Telegraph (2013b) "Nicolas Maduro Wins Venezuela Election by
Tiny Margin," April 15th.

The Daily Telegraph (2013c) "Ghost of Hugo Chavez in the Driving Seat as
Venezuela Votes," April 12th.

Dominguez, F. (2011) "Venezuela's Opposition: Desperately Seeking to Over-
throw Chavez," in Dominguez, F., Lievesley, G. and Ludlum, S. (eds.) *Right-
Wing Politics in the New Latin America: Reaction and Revolt*, London: Zed
Books.

Duno-Gottberg, L. (2009) "Social Images of Anti-Apocalypse: Bikers and the
Representation of Popular Politics in Venezuela," *A Contra Corriente*, 6:2,
pp. 144–172.

Duno-Gottberg, L. (2011) "The Color of Mobs: Racial Politics, Ethnopop-
ulism, and Representation in the Chavez Era," in Smidle, D. and Hellinger,
D. (eds.) *Venezuela's Bolivarian Democracy: Participation, Politics, and
Culture Under Chavez*, Durham: Duke University Press.

Embassy of Venezuela (2012) "Venezuela's 2012 Presidential Elections," September, http://eeuu.embajada.gob.ve/index.php?option=com_content&view=article&id=216&Itemid=3&lang=en

European Parliament (2005) "Election Observation of Parliamentary Elections in Venezuela, 2nd-6th December 2005," www.europarl.europa.eu/intcoop/election_observation/missions/2004-2009/20051204_venezuela_parliamentary.pdf

European Union Election Observation Mission (2006) "Final Report: Presidential Elections in Venezuela, 2006," http://eeas.europa.eu/eueom/pdf/missions/moe_ue_venezuela_2006_final_eng.pdf

Fernandes, S. (2010) *Who Can Stop the Drums? Urban Social Movements in Chavez's Venezuela*, London: Duke University Press.

Financial Times (2012) "Venezuela Awaits David and Goliath Contest," October 5th, www.ft.com/cms/s/0/d921292c-0edb-11e2-ba6b-00144feabdc0.html

Gobierno de España (2017) "Comunicado del Gobierno tras las elecciones en Venezuela," April 16th, www.lamoncloa.gob.es/serviciosdeprensa/notasprensa/maec/Paginas/2013/160413ComunVenezuela.aspx

The Guardian (2013) "Hugo Chavez Showed That the West's Ways Aren't Always Best," March 11th.

The Independent (2013a) "Anointed Heir Faces Competition for the Poisoned Chalice," March 7th.

Kitzberger, P. (2012) "The Media Politics of Latin America's Leftist Governments," *Journal of Politics in Latin America*, 4:3, pp. 123–139.

Latinobarómetro (1995–2015) *Latinobarómetro Reports*, www.Latinobarómetro.org/

Lovato, R. (2014) "Why the Media Are Giving a Free Pass to Venezuela's Neo-Fascist Creeps," *The Nation*, April 1st, www.thenation.com/article/179125/why-media-are-giving-free-pass-venezuelas-neo-fascist-creeps

Lupien, P. (2013) "The Media in Venezuela and Bolivia: Attacking the 'Bad Left' From Below," *Latin American Perspectives*, 40, pp. 226–246.

Miami Herald (2013a) "Hugo Chavez Is Dead but His Vote Machine Lives," April 13th.

Miami Herald (2013b) "Outcome of Venezuelan Vote Leaves Future Cloudy," April 15th.

Miami Herald (2013c)"Venezuelans Head to Vote Amid Echoes of 2002 Coup," April 12th.

Miami Herald (2013d) "Venezuela Campaign Ends With Massive Rallies," April 11th.

Miami Herald (2013e) "Maduro to Take Power Amid Questions and Protests," April 18th.

Miami Herald (2013f) "Seven Dead in Venezuela Election Protests," April 16th.

MUD (2012) "Lineamientos para el Programa de Gobierno de Unidad Nacional (2013–2019)," January 23rd, http://static.telesurtv.net/filesOnRFS/opinion/2015/12/09/mud_government_plan.pdf

Naím, M. (2014) "The Tragedy of Venezuela," *The Atlantic*, February 25th, www.theatlantic.com/international/archive/2014/02/the-tragedy-of-venezuela/284062/

NBC (2012) "Center-left Progressive Henrique Capriles Set to Challenge Hugo Chavez," February 13th, www.nbcnews.com/id/46364316/ns/world_news-venezuela/t/center-left-progressive-henrique-capriles-set-challenge-hugo-chavez/

New York Times (2002) "Chavez's Second Chance," April 18th.

New York Times (2013a) "Even in Death, Chavez Is a Powerful Presence," April 9th.

New York Times (2013b) "Venezuela Gives Chavez Protégé Narrow Victory," April 15th.

Padgett, T. (2012) "Candidate Capriles: Could This Man Defeat Venezuela's Hugo Chavez?" *Time*, January 25th, http://world.time.com/2012/01/25/candidate-capriles-could-this-man-defeat-venezuelas-hugo-chavez/

The Real News (2012) "Jimmy Carter Says 'Election Process in Venezuela Is the Best in the World," *The Real News*, October 5th, http://therealnews.com/t2/index.php?option=com_content&task=view&id=767&Itemid=74&jumival=8935

Rosnick, D. and Weisbrot, M. (2007) "Political Forecasting? The IMF's Flawed Growth Projections for Argentina and Venezuela," *CEPR*, April, www.cepr.net/index.php/publications/reports/political-forecasting-the-imfs-flawed-growth-projections-for-argentina-and-venezuela

Sanchez, G. (2007) *Cuba and Venezuela: An Insight Into Two Revolutions*, Melbourne: Ocean Press.

The Times (2013a) "Embalmed Chavez to Be Permanent Exhibit in 'Museum of the Revolution,'" March 8th.

The Times (2013b) "The 'Chosen One' Puts a Curse on Those Who Won't Keep the Faith," April 8th.

Tinker-Salas, M. (2015) *Venezuela: What Everyone Needs to Know*, Oxford: Oxford University Press.

Trinkunas, H. and McCoy, J. (1999) "Observation of the 1998 Venezuelan Elections," *The Carter Center*, www.cartercenter.org/documents/1151.pdf

UNASUR (2013) "Declaración del Consejo de Jefes y Jefas de Estado y de Gobierno de UNASUR," *Presidencia de la República del Perú*, April 19th, www.presidencia.gob.pe/declaracion-del-consejo-de-jefes-y-jefas-de-estado-y-de-gobierno-de-la-union-de-naciones-suramericanas-unasur

Washington Post (2013a) "Venezuela's Reckoning," April 12th.

Washington Post (2013b) "Venezuela May Lose Freewheeling News Outlet," April 14th.

Weisbrot, M. and Ruttenberg, T. (2010) "Television in Venezuela: Who Dominates the Media?" *CEPR*, December, www.cepr.net/index.php/publications/reports/who-dominates-the-media-in-venezuela

5   The 2014 *guarimbas*

In early 2014, Venezuela was gripped by opposition street demonstrations (*guarimbas*) against Nicolas Maduro, which made worldwide headlines and went viral on social media. There was a very wide range of interpretations of the events. The eight key points of contention identified were the following:

1   Is this a legitimate protest or a coup attempt?
2   Who is demonstrating?
3   Why are they demonstrating?
4   Do they have links to outsiders, specifically the American government?
5   How violent are they and who is responsible for the violence?
6   What has been the government's response?
7   How widespread are the demonstrations?
8   Are the demonstrations designed to overthrow government?

Competing explanations

Presented below are two major explanations of the *guarimbas*, together with a range of views from other academics.

The anti-government frame

This end of the spectrum sees the *guarimbas* as a spontaneous, grass-roots (Corrales, 2014a) and extremely widespread citizen's protest movement, encompassing a wide range of people (Corrales, 2014b), but led by "unbelievably brave" students facing down a "budding military dictatorship" (Toro, 2014b). Naím (2014) argues the protestors were demonstrating against disastrous government mismanagement of the economy, which led to inflation, crime and food shortages, but, due to the government's repression, morphed into a protest against a "repressive regime that treats them as mortal enemies" and that the idea protest leaders are in league with the CIA is laughable. While Toro (2014b) concedes the protestors have been guilty of violence, including shooting police and beheading passers-by, he contends that the government and its paramilitary gangs have been responsible for a great deal more, resulting in a "tropical pogrom" (2014a).

The Chavista *frame*

In contrast, the government and pro-government media categorize the events not as a protest but rather a "right-wing rampage" aimed at overthrowing Maduro illegally (Telesur, 2015b), a concerted effort by the far-right, working closely with Washington, to overthrow the government. For the *chavistas*, those protesting are not a grassroots group of citizens but a small group of rich students from elite universities and the light-skinned privileged elites who are conducting a terroristic campaign of violence to intimidate the population into submission, shooting journalists, attacking food stores, setting national parks ablaze, attacking ambulances and burning doctors alive, even setting light to a kindergarten where nearly 100 children lay frightened (Ibid). In April, Maduro claimed the damages caused by the "rampage" totaled US$15 billion (Pearson and Mallett-Outtrim, 2015). *Chavistas* accept there were cases of serious misconduct by the authorities but argue their response was, overall, "amazingly restrained" (Ibid).

Other academic opinions

Between these two extremes there was a range of academic opinions. Buxton (2014) characterized the demonstrations as violent actions carried out by light-skinned students from elitist institutions who were defending the *ancien regime* and their own privilege. Furthermore, she claims a section of the student movement in Venezuela is deeply embedded with Washington. Student leader Yon Goicoechea was awarded the Cato Institute's US$500,000 Milton Friedman Prize for advancing liberty for his role in organizing previous anti-government demonstrations and was a member of Leopoldo Lopez's political party. Ellner (2014a) noted that provoking violence and blaming it on the enemy is a "time-worn tactic" of the opposition, using it, for instance, during the coup of 2002 (as discussed in Chapter 2). He stated that the protesters actions were "terrorism", cataloging the long list of attacks against civilians, such as the destruction of the Caracas Metro and 90 Metro buses with hundreds of passengers attacked, the complete demolition of a campus of the military school UNEFA and attacks on the

Housing Ministry, state-owned food distributors and 162 Cuban doctors (Ibid). However, McCoy (2014) noted that the government was far from blameless and was guilty of fomenting a polarized situation where there was no room for middle ground. Smilde (2014) went further, claiming that it was the "wild" government repression of the protesters that greatly increased their size and engulfed the country in chaos.

Reactions from international actors

International reaction contrasted greatly. Many Latin American and Caribbean states and institutions immediately backed the government and condemned what they saw as a US-backed coup attempt.

> "On behalf of the Bolivian people, we send our energy and support to the courageous Venezuelan people and president Nicolas Maduro" announced President Evo Morales, "this coup attempt is being financed from abroad, by the United States".
>
> (Cadena Agramonte, 2014)

Mercosur also rejected the "criminal actions" of the *guarimba* leaders (AVN, 2015) while UNASUR expressed its solidarity with the government and the victims of the opposition's violence and rejected the right-wing's attempt to destabilize the country (Rosas, 2014). The EU advised that the only way out of the situation was through peaceful dialogue (European Parliament News, 2014). British Foreign Minister William Hague said that he was "very concerned" about "the arrests of opposition activists" and called on the government to uphold freedom of the press and opinion (*El Nacional*, 2014). Meanwhile, there was strong condemnation of the government in the United States, with former Vice-President Joe Biden accusing it of,

> Confronting peaceful protesters with force and in some cases with armed vigilantes; limiting the freedoms of press and assembly necessary for legitimate political debate; demonizing and arresting political opponents; and dramatically tightening restrictions on the media.

And Biden said that instead of working on dialogue, Maduro had tried to "distract" Venezuelans from internal issues by "concocting totally false and outlandish conspiracy theories about the United States" (Bajak, 2014).

Senators immediately began discussing sanctions on Venezuela and President Obama himself declared a "national emergency" with respect to the "extraordinary threat to the national security and foreign policy of the United States posed by the situation in Venezuela" (White House, 2015), which were subsequently extended. Since 2014, the US has been in a formal state of emergency due to the actions of the Venezuelan government.

These reactions would be worth noting as we analyze the media's framing of events.

Empirical evidence

In all, 43 people died in the 2014 *guarimbas*. The number of pro- and anti-government deaths is disputed but the range of statistical evidence indicates that they are approximately equal (Johnston, 2014). There were also a number citizens killed who were not affiliated with either side. However, media watchdog group Fairness and Accuracy in Reporting stated:

> The presence of the protest barricades appears to be the most common cause of deaths: individuals shot while attempting to clear the opposition street blockades, automobile accidents caused by the presence of the barricades, and several incidents attributed to the opposition stringing razor wire across streets near the barricades.
>
> (Hart, 2014)

Leaked cables (Main and Beeton, 2015) have shown that the US government funded a number of the leaders of the *guarimbas* and that funding for Venezuelan anti-government activists increased by 80 percent from 2012 to 2014. The cables also show that the US State Department was well aware that many of the leaders had exceptionally violent pasts. For instance, Nixon Moreno had led a crowd to the state capital of Merida to *lynch the governor* in 2002, and later was accused of murder and of the rape of a police officer, yet it continued to train and support him (Beeton et al. 2015: 525–526).

Evidence strongly suggests the demonstrations were designed from the beginning as a coup, an attempt to forcefully remove Maduro. Inside Venezuela, opposition leaders were open about their intentions. When asked how long he planned the demonstrations to go on, the movement's leader, Leopoldo Lopez replied, "until Maduro goes" (Tinker-Salas, 2014). Indeed, the name the movement gave itself was

"*La Salida*" or "the exit" [of Maduro]. In October 2013 Lopez gave a speech in the United States, where he said:

> We have to hurry the exit of the government. . . . Nicolas Maduro must go out sooner than later from the Venezuelan government. Nicolas Maduro and all his supporters . . . from my point of view, the method is secondary, what is important is the determination to reach our goals at any cost.

During an interview at the time, he was asked when the opposition protests would end. "When we manage to remove those who govern us," he replied (Fuchs and Vivanco, 2015).

The violence of the protesters, particularly the beheadings of passing civilians Elvis Rafael Duran and Delia Elena Lobo strongly challenge the idea that the demonstrations represented a respectable, peaceful protest against inflation, crime and food shortages, as some anti-Chavez scholars believe. Furthermore, the targets of attack by the protesters: kindergartens, universities, health clinics, more than 160 Cuban doctors (some who protesters attempted to burn alive) (Ellner, 2014b), the Caracas Metro, etc. all have a clear political message: the buildings and institutions targeted were representations of the flagship programs in education, health, transport, etc. of the missions, the epitomes of the collectivist, social-democratic state the government had been trying to build since 1999.

It should also be noted that the problems of crime, inflation and food shortages mentioned as reasons for protesting are issues that least affect the wealthy and disproportionately affect the poor. For instance, 70 percent of homicides in Caracas occur in the poor El Libertador municipality while less than one percent occur in rich Chacao (Humphrey and Valverde, 2014: 157). Yet the polling company IVAD found a strong class correlation to supporting the *guarimbas*, with those from higher socioeconomic backgrounds much more likely to approve of the actions (Nagel, 2014). Empirical evidence showed the protests *did not* grip the country, shutting down cities, but occurred in 18 of the country's 335 municipalities, primarily affluent, opposition-controlled districts and *did not* spread to other areas (Tinker-Salas, 2015: 213). Light-skinned private university students led the protests; *The New York Times* (2014h) remarked that the poor were notable in their absence. Thus, the people most affected by crime and violence were the *least* likely to protest while those least affected by the issues raised were the *most* likely to protest.

When asked themselves by polling firm International Consulting Services, 11.6 percent of the Venezuelan people agreed with the

Table 5.1 Do you agree or disagree with the *guarimbas?* Venezuela, Noticias24 (2014)

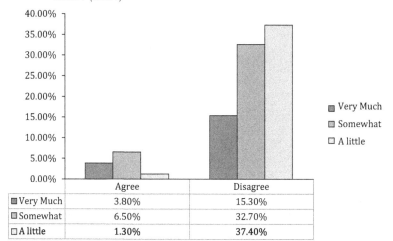

	Agree	Disagree
■ Very Much	3.80%	15.30%
▨ Somewhat	6.50%	32.70%
□ A little	1.30%	37.40%

guarimbas, while 85.4 percent of those asked were against them (Noticias24, 2014).

Although the survey found support for Maduro was low, another polling firm, Hinterlaces, found that 87% of Venezuelans were against the violent demonstrations, 79% felt that any form of protest was making the country worse and 86% agreed with the electoral results and rejected "unconstitutional shortcuts" (Ibid). An anti-*chavista* polling firm, Datanalisis, found that although demonstrations that originally had the support of most of the population; by April 2014, two-thirds of Venezuelans were against them (Nagel, 2014). The opposition's leader, Henrique Capriles, *did not* support the *guarimbas* and tried to start peaceful dialogue with Maduro as they were going on, effectively shunning the more extreme movement within the opposition, led by Lopez.

Analysis

Protests, riots or a coup attempt?

A sample of newspaper articles covering the protests was taken. All articles containing the word "Venezuela" covering the unrest from February 1st to May 1st were included, except for *The Miami Herald,*

Table 5.2 2014 *guarimbas*: protests or a coup?

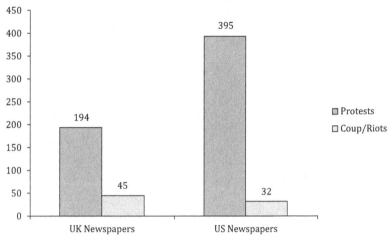

which was from February 1st to March 1st. As before, this was done to prevent *The Herald* from swamping the survey, as it publishes more articles on Venezuela than other newspapers.

The primary question of whether the *guarimbas* constituted a coup or a protest will be dealt with first. This is an important point of contention as the framing of the events as a protest or as a riot conveys a great difference in legitimacy. "The 2011 London Protests" conveys a great deal more legitimacy to the event as does "The 2011 London Riots".

In total, the British newspapers identified the actions as protests 194 times and a coup or riots 45 times. The American press identified them 395 times as protests and 32 times as a coup or riots.

There was a strong tendency in both countries to identify the *guarimbas* as a protest rather than as riots or a coup attempt. The UK media identified it as a protest at a nearly 5:1 ratio but the tendency was exceptionally strong in the United States, where that figure was over 12:1. Typical examples of how the affair was identified as a protest include the following:

> Death toll from Venezuela street protests rises to 18; Anti-government protests continue to Caracas and across Venezuela.
>
> (*The Daily Telegraph*, 2014a)

Venezuela's crackdown on anti-government street protests is a threat to democracy across Latin America.

(*The Guardian*, 2014a)

Faced with a government that systematically equates protest with treason, people have been protesting in defense of the very right to protest.

(*The New York Times*, 2014a)

However, the considerable quantitative inequality is not an accurate reflection of the true level of disparity in the articles, as it does not take into consideration the *quality* of the references. Virtually all of the articles framed the *guarimbas* overall as protests, and often emphasized their peaceful and respectable nature while very few took the notion that these were violent riots or a coup attempt seriously. A small minority of reports, mostly in *The Independent* and *The Guardian* had any articles whatsoever doing as such. It was presented as a matter of fact that the events were protests being repressed by the government, thus mirroring the line taken by the US and UK governments. When mentioned at all, the idea that this constituted a coup attempt was often stated as an accusation in the mouth of a Venezuelan official, from a supposedly repressive government that the newspapers have been undermining and attacking for years, as seen throughout this study. For example:

The protests, which started last Saturday in the state of Merida, were initially led by students demanding the release of classmates jailed after earlier protests and an attack on the governor's residence in Tachira state . . . but supporters of the government . . . see the demonstrations as a desperate push to oust Maduro.

(*The Guardian*, 2014b)

This example was quantitatively coded as one framing as a protest and one as a coup. However, it is presented as *a matter of fact* that the events constitute protests about crime and economic issues whereas the idea that this was an attempt to overthrow President Maduro is presented merely as *an assertion* that exists only in the mind of supporters of a government the article itself characterizes as repressive and incompetent. It should be noted that this framing was among the *more sympathetic* to the government found in the sample, as it at least states that there is an alternative viewpoint. The majority of the articles *did not consider the idea that these were anything else except legitimate protests*. Therefore, most readers were not even exposed to the idea that there was any debate over the issue, let alone that the balance of evidence pointed to a different conclusion to those given in what they were reading. Other articles were more dismissive (emphasis added):

> Mr Maduro has gone out of his way to inflame tension by making *wild allegations* that the protests are an attempted coup by the far Right with backing from the United States.
>
> (*The Times*, 2014a)

> The government, for its part, is *sticking to the old script*: Venezuela is falling victim to a fascist *conspiracy* cooked up by American officials who are terrified of its revolutionary aspirations . . . *The claim is outlandish*, yet its ceaseless repetition reveals that to the Venezuelan government, all dissent is treason.
>
> (*The New York Times*, 2014a)

Phrases such as "wild allegations", "sticking to the old script" and "outlandish" demonstrate the tone of the media and what their opinion of these allegations is. Yet these examples all counted towards the "coup" identification total. But these were not wild allegations. As highlighted previously, US government documents prove it was

Table 5.3 The 2014 *guarimbas*: a protest or a coup? Identifications in selected media

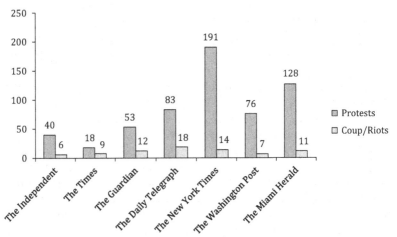

training and funding *guarimba* leaders to oppose the government and to "penetrate" *chavismo*. Thus, the majority of the articles took exactly the same line and shared the same tone and *even the same word choices* as former Vice-President Biden, who immediately supported the *guarimbas*.

As stated above, both countries' newspapers displayed a pronounced tendency to describe the events of 2014 as protests, although the American newspapers did so overwhelmingly. This contradicted the stance taken by Latin American governments *and even the guarimba leaders themselves*, who, as shown previously, were explicit in their intentions to oust Maduro from office. Thus, all major actors in Venezuelan society agreed the *guarimbas'* goal was to get rid of Maduro. Yet the media treated this idea as marginal, at best, and usually as risible or even non-existent. This was despite interviewing protesters *who told them that that was exactly what they were trying to do*, as can be seen in the following quotes.

> We are urging the international community to assist us in ridding Venezuela of this government.
>
> (*The Miami Herald*, 2014a)

> 'The fate of Castro-ism may be at play in Venezuela,' Mr. Pardo said. 'What we were not able to topple in Cuba, we may be able to topple there.'
>
> (*The New York Times*, 2014b)

Who is protesting and why?

Despite the pronounced class aspect to the protests, which was remarked upon immediately by respected commentators (Buxton, 2014) and the government (*The Daily Telegraph*, 2014b), a comparatively small one in seven articles from the 2014 sample mentioned that there was anything that could mean class was a factor in the makeup of the protesters. The sampling was particularly generous, including any comment or statement that could be construed to note that there was a class aspect to the protest, even if it were only to immediately repudiate the idea, as seen below:

> While the protests are strongest in middle class areas, they have sporadically spread to poorer neighbourhoods which are traditionally aligned with the Socialist government.
>
> (*The Daily Telegraph*, 2014c)

Today, large rallies continue in the middle-class neighborhoods of all the main cities . . . the protests have spread from middle-class neighborhoods to the slums.

(*The New York Times*, 2014c)

In total, there were 33 references in 17 articles to the high class-correlation of the protests. British newspapers were more likely to mention this theme (10 of 52 articles) than American (7 of 72). Sometimes the mentioning of class was put in the form of an accusation from the government, as in this example:

The protesters (which the government insists are spoilt rich kids and saboteurs in the pay of foreign powers, who have nothing to do with 'the people').

(*The Daily Telegraph*, 2014b)

In addition to the limited discussion about the class aspect to the protests, many newspapers not only rejected this, but put forward the opposite analysis, that the protests were widespread across class lines, such as in this quote:

Since then the street actions have mushroomed to include people from all walks of life who have seen their salaries evaporate under the heat of inflation.

(*The Guardian*, 2014c)

This study also monitored the explanations offered as to why people were in the streets. They were split into four categories: economic concerns, concerns over crime, a coup attempt or other explanations. These "other explanations" were primarily government human rights abuses and the rape of a student on campus. Typical ways of presenting the explanations for protesting included the following two examples:

Protesters who are angered by spiraling crime, high inflation, shortages, and a crackdown on freedom of speech.

(*The Times*, 2014b).

Street demonstrations by students and average citizens fed up with soaring inflation, shortages of basic goods, one of the world's highest murder rates and a government whose only response has been to shout senseless populist slogans.

(*The Washington Post*, 2014a).

Table 5.4 Why are there street demonstrations? Explanations offered by sampled newspapers

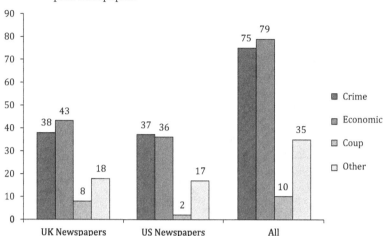

Overall, crime was identified 75 times as a trigger for the protests, economic problems 79 times and other reasons 37 times in 17 articles. A coup attempt was identified a comparatively small ten times as the reason for the *guarimbas, despite guarimba leader Leopoldo Lopez continually stating that the objective of the protests was to depose President Maduro* (Tinker-Salas, 2014; Fuchs and Vivanco, 2015).

Links to the American government

Of the 124 articles in 2014, around a third, 44, mentioned the possibility of US government involvement with the *guarimbas.*

As before, however, only looking at the quantitative data gives an inaccurate picture of the situation because very often the idea of US involvement was brought up only to ridicule the notion, as exemplified in the following examples (emphasis added):

> Mr. Maduro's *predictable response* in the government-controlled news media has been to blame it all on "fascists" and the United States.
>
> (*The New York Times*, 2014d)

> The Maduro government blames the protests on 'fascists' and, *of course*, the United States. He ordered the expulsion of three US diplomats, claiming *disingenuously* that these consular officers organized the protests.
>
> (*The Miami Herald*, 2014b)

Table 5.5 Mentioning of possible US Government involvement in 2014 protests, UK and US newspapers

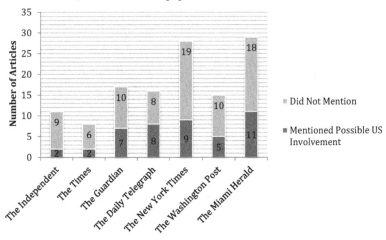

All of these sorts of examples counted towards US involvement. The second is particularly notable as the article was written by Charles Shapiro, the US Ambassador to Venezuela in 2002 and a major actor in the coup attempt to remove Chavez that year! (See Chapter 2). There was a greater tendency among the right-wing press (*The Daily Telegraph*) and the US press to treat the notion as "absurd" (*The Miami Herald*, 2014c), despite the fact that released official documents strongly implicate the US government in one aborted coup against the government and that leaked documents showed the US government increasing its effort to "penetrate" and "divide" *chavismo* in order to produce regime change (Beeton et al., 2015: 518). One notable exception to this trend was Seumas Milne, who wrote four articles in April for *The Guardian*, which treated US involvement seriously and took a critical stance towards the *guarimbas*. Without Milne's articles, *The Guardian's* coverage would have been similar to that of other newspapers. Thus, the virtually the entire gamut of the media took exactly the same position as the US government; that its involvement in the *guarimbas* was nothing but an "outlandish conspiracy theory", as Joe Biden said.

Who was responsible for the violence?

In total, there were 207 separate identifications that the government or pro-government groups were behind the violence and 90 identifications that the opposition protestors were responsible.

Table 5.6 Who is responsible for the violence? Identifications in selected newspapers

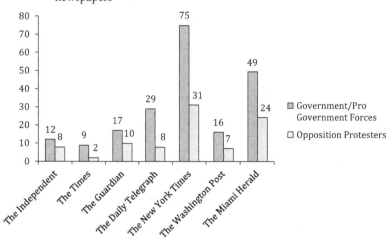

As seen before, the left-of-centre British newspapers allowed for some degree of nuance to their positions, with some content sympathetic to the government. However, they still displayed a tendency to identify the *chavistas* as those primarily guilty. The other newspapers showed a stronger tendency to do so.

Furthermore, the quality of the identifications of violence differed greatly. The left-of-centre UK papers were worried about authoritarian repression:

> White House spokesman, Jay Carney, voiced concern that the government was using security forces and armed gangs to break up peaceful demonstrations.
>
> (*The Independent*, 2014a)

Whereas the American papers reported on full-scale massacres of innocents:

> Many Latin American experts in Washington agree that the Obama Administration cannot look the other way as peaceful protesters are massacred by government-supported armed thugs.
>
> (*The Miami Herald*, 2014d)

In contrast, in 58 of 124 articles was there any mention of opposition violence. As before, when the opposition was connected to something negative, it very often came in the form of an accusation in the mouth of a Venezuelan official, whose credibility has been undermined through years of negative reporting. For example:

> Both sides blame each other for the bloodshed.
> (*The Daily Telegraph*, 2014c)

> Mr Maduro had blamed more than 50 deaths in a fortnight on the 'fascist' opposition.
> (*The Times*, 2014c)

But the articles often undermined even these weak accusations (emphasis added):

> The government *quickly* accused Mr. López of being responsible for the unrest and the deaths.
> (*The New York Times*, 2014e)

> Mr. Maduro *immediately* blamed a prominent opposition leader, Leopoldo López, for the violence.
> (*The New York Times*, 2014f)

The emphasis of accusing someone immediately connotes a sense of hastiness or a knee-jerk reaction based upon political expediency, rather than one based on evidence. Thus, the veracity of the claims appears especially dubious. Government accusations of opposition violence were often immediately met with statements that said the government had no evidence whatsoever for their allegations. Furthermore, the scale of the violence mentioned in connection to either side differed greatly. The violence that the opposition was accused of tended to be relatively minor, such as smashing windows or throwing Molotov cocktails while the government was guilty of a full-scale crackdown on basic liberties. Thus, *The Guardian* claimed the protesters had "only sticks and rocks" (2014d) while the government had "army tank, helicopters and paratrooper regiments" (2014e). This is all despite watchdog groups identifying the barricades themselves as the primary cause of death.

Only two articles of 124, from Seumas Milne and Owen Jones, mentioned that the protesters had beheaded two innocent passers-by as part of the *guarimbas*. This cannot be because it was not known, as it was widely reported inside Venezuela and on social media. It cannot be because the information was not pertinent, as other deaths

Table 5.7 Respectable or violent protesters? Identifications in selected newspapers

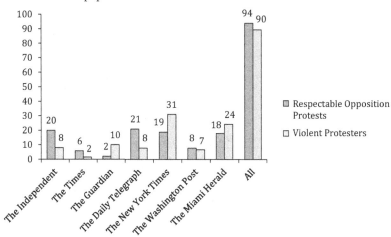

were reported. And it certainly cannot be because the story was not newsworthy; the events provided a particularly easy story and striking headline. Furthermore, the murders happened on February 21st, in the first month of the survey, giving the newspapers months to include it. Events such as the attacks on universities were barely mentioned, while the attacks on kindergartens and on Cuban doctors were not reported whatsoever. Opposition protesters who died, such as Genesis Carmona, were regularly named and discussed in detail; many stories were based around them. In contrast, government supporters or people killed by the opposition, such as those beheaded, were not.

Indeed, the protesters at the *guarimbas* were often identified as paragons of virtue, as peaceful model citizens standing up for their rights. This was more common than the violent framing, as the graph below shows. One *Daily Telegraph* (2014d) article described them as "family matriarchs carrying bibles after mass" staging peaceful protest against repression being met with "barrages of tear gas".

How widespread were the demonstrations?

The study tracked whether the articles identified the *guarimbas* as isolated and or unpopular or widespread and or serious. As noted above, while certainly not insignificant, they were notably isolated, appearing in a limited number of Venezuela's districts, most of them in conspicuously wealthy, white areas. From a peak in February, the

Table 5.8 Identifications of the demonstrations: isolated and unpopular or
widespread and serious

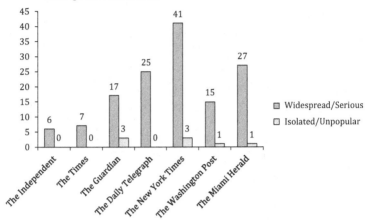

demonstrations petered out, leaving a hardcore of students in isolated
pockets. Furthermore, multiple surveys have shown they were decidedly unpopular. However, the media showed a distinct preference to
treat the protests as widespread and serious. "Hundreds of thousands
of Venezuelans have taken to the streets," (*The Miami Herald*, 2014c)
"all over Venezuela", (*The Daily Telegraph*, 2014b) actions that have
"rocked their country", (*The Washington Post*, 2014b) creating a
"crisis" (*The Times*, 2014d) that is "the loudest things have gotten in
a decade" (*The Washington Post*, 2014c).

With regard to the Isolated or Unpopular frame, very little was
offered. There was near unanimity among outlets that the protests
were widespread and serious, despite the evidence strongly suggesting that the *guarimbas* were unpopular and markedly limited in their
scope. *The Miami Herald* (2014e) did mention that the street protests were "sporadic" while *The Washington Post* (2014d) quoted
pollster Luis Vicente Leon saying "not all the country is protesting".
The majority of *The Guardian*'s dissenting opinion was once again
supplied by Seumas Milne, who noted that the demonstrations were
overwhelmingly in white, middle-class areas (2014f). This amounted
to the majority of information in the entire sample of 124 articles suggesting the *guarimbas* were not countrywide and a serious, popular
challenge to the government.

Overall, both the British and American press displayed a strong tendency towards presenting the *guarimbas* as widespread, respectable
protests against an authoritarian government. They presented minority opinions on exceptionally contentious issues as facts while rarely

mentioning the opposing, majority opinion. When it was mentioned, it was rarely taken seriously. While some newspapers, notably *The Guardian*, had a small amount of space for dissenting opinions, the overall picture built up across every newspaper studied jarred violently with the empirical data available. It also jarred strongly with the coverage of the protests in other outlets. For instance, *RT*, a Russian-based network, took a critical stance to the protests, as can be seen by looking at their headlines:

> "It's simply about regime change, not improving Venezuela's economy."
>
> (March 25th)

> "Protesters in Venezuela 'don't seem to have clear demands,'"
>
> (February 26th)

> "'Venezuela is low-hanging fruit for US,'"
>
> (February 25th)

> "S. American leaders call for peace in Venezuela amid violent protests."
>
> (March 8th)

> "Venezuela coup? Gunfire, clashes as 3 dead in violent Caracas protest"
>
> (February 13th)

In many of its news articles and op-eds, *RT* reported the reaction to the *guarimbas* from Latin American leaders, took seriously the idea that the affair was a US-backed attempt to force President Maduro out, while simultaneously presenting the contrary viewpoint of Lopez and the protesters. Unlike the newspapers in the survey, *RT* is state-funded, receiving funding from the Russian government, which, in recent years, has enjoyed a largely cordial relationship with Venezuela. In contrast, the newspapers in this survey, particularly the American ones, are based in a country whose government is entirely hostile to the Bolivarian project. Therefore, journalists and editors of *RT* do not have to consider flak from their governments that could undermine their jobs, or even their outlet's existence if they present Venezuela positively or neutrally. Furthermore, unlike *RT*, the newspapers in this survey rely on advertising from transnational corporations for the large majority of their funding. The Venezuelan government espouses an ideology (twenty-first-century socialism) contrary to the interests of these corporations (neoliberalism). Consequentially, *RT* journalists and editors have no reason to provide content that conforms to and promotes the worldview of transnational corporations. Thus, journalists at *RT* are relatively free to present Venezuela however they choose. However, they would perhaps not feel free to present the Russian government or issues critical to the Russian state negatively.

It was evidently possible for *RT* to present a nuanced or even critical content. If *RT*, Jones and Milne had access to relevant factual information then the specific framing of the Venezuela protests cannot be explained due to a lack of information. The newspapers systematically presented the protests in the fashion most favourable to their governments, owners and advertisers, with nuanced or critical opinions pushed to the margins. By and large, the newspapers presented repeated opposition talking points as matters of fact while ignoring or deriding government counterclaims and followed the line put forward by the White House and by Lopez.

In fact, it was often virtually impossible to distinguish between the newspapers in this sample and the Venezuelan opposition's position. Lopez was given an op-ed in *The New York Times* (2014g), where he gave his side of the story, how over the last 15 years, Venezuela had become intolerable, due to government incompetence and repression, that had left the country with "one of the highest murder rates in the Western Hemisphere", a "57 percent inflation rate" and a "scarcity of basic goods" unseen outside of wartime. He claimed there was an "equally oppressive political climate" where he urged Venezuelans to peacefully use their rights to protest and free speech but that the government killed three people protesting.

The New York Times and *Washington Post* editorial boards released their own analysis of events. *The Times* (2014d) claimed:

> People hit the streets – driven to despair by rampant crime, including one of the highest murder rates in the world; chronic shortages of basic staples, often including milk and toilet paper; raging inflation, which last year reached an annual rate of 56.2 percent; and frequent blackouts.

While claiming Maduro's "predictable response" was to blame it on fascists and the US. *The Washington Post* (2014a) characterized the *guarimbas* as:

> Street demonstrations by students and average citizens fed up with soaring inflation, shortages of basic goods, one of the world's

highest murder rates and a government whose only response has been to shout senseless populist slogans.

It also repeated the contentious claim that the demonstrators were killed by gunmen "likely affiliated" with the government and described Lopez as "courageously surrendering" the authorities.

If we compare Lopez's position to those of the newspapers' editorial boards, we see that they are functionally identical, including many of the same talking points (inflation) and turns of phrase (one of the highest murder rates in the world) and accusations about the government being responsible for the deaths. If we removed the by-line, there would be no discernable difference between the opposition's position and supposedly balanced outlets.

Across our five samples, we have seen how the media have consistently taken positions critical of government, often despite the large weight of easily verifiable evidence suggesting the opposite conclusions. Now it is time to turn our attention to *why* this is happening.

References

AVN (2015) "Mercosur Summit Reaffirmed Full and Absolute Support to Venezuela in the Region," July 20th, www.avn.info.ve/contenido/mercosur-summit-reaffirmed-full-and-absolute-support-venezuela-region

Bajak, F. (2014) "Joe Biden: Venezuela Situation Is Alarming," *The Huffington Post*, March 10th, www.huffingtonpost.com/2014/03/09/joe-biden-venezuela_n_4931069.html

Beeton, D., Johnston, J. and Main, A. (2015) "Venezuela," in Wikileaks (ed.) *Wikileaks: The World According to the US Empire*, London: Verso.

Bracchi Roa, L. (2014) "Venezuela: How Photos Get Manipulated," *Latin American Bureau*, February 23rd, http://lab.org.uk/venezuela-how-photos-get-manipulated

Buxton, J. (2014) "Venezuela: The Real Significance of the Student Protests," *Latin American Bureau*, February 20th, http://lab.org.uk/venezuela-%E2%80%93-student-protests

Cadena Agramonte (2014) "US Is Trying to Destroy Chavez' Legacy, President Evo Morales Says," February 18th, www.cadenagramonte.cu/english/index.php/show/articles/17167:us-is-trying-to-destroy-chavez-legacy-president-evo-morales-says

Corrales, J. (2014a) "Why Venezuela's Student Protesters Have Already Won," *The Washington Post*, February 28th, www.washingtonpost.com/opinions/why-venezuelas-student-protesters-have-already-won/2014/02/28/b4f94d2a-a009-11e3-9ba6-800d1192d08b_story.html

Corrales, J. (2014b) "Venezuela's Middle Ground," *Foreign Policy*, April 22nd, http://foreignpolicy.com/2014/04/22/venezuelas-middle-ground/

The Daily Telegraph (2014a) "Death Toll From Venezuela Street Protests Rises to 18," March 1st.

The Daily Telegraph (2014b) "People Are Dying: Should the Band Play on?" February 27th.

The Daily Telegraph (2014c) "Venezuela Orders Troops Into Border City Amid Fierce Clashes," February 21st.

The Daily Telegraph (2014d) "Venezuelan Troops Tear Through Border City to Crush Student Protest in Cradle of Uprising," April 1st.

El Nacional (2014) "Reino Unido Preocupado por Detenciones de Oposición en Venezuela," February 18th.

Ellner, S. (2014a) "Terrorism in Venezuela and Its Accomplices," *Venezuelanalysis*, May 15th, http://venezuelanalysis.com/analysis/10684

Ellner, S. (2014b) "Opposition Violence: A Time-Worn Tactic Played out in Venezuela," *Alborada*, February 13th, www.alborada.net/ellner-venezuela-130214

European Parliament News (2014) "Venezuela: Peaceful and Respectful Dialogue Only Way out of the Crisis, MEPs Say," February27th, www.europarl.europa.eu/news/en/news-room/20140225IPR36958/Venezuela-peaceful-and-respectful-dialogue-only-way-out-of-the-crisis-MEPs-say

Fuchs, G. and Vivanco, P. (2015) "The Distorted 'Democracy' of Leopoldo Lopez," *Telesur*, January 29th, www.telesurtv.net/english/analysis/The-Distorted-Democracy-of-Leopoldo-Lopez-20150129-0022.html

The Guardian (2014a) "Venezuela Protest Crackdown Threatens Region's Democracy, Warns Vargas Llosa," April 10th.

The Guardian (2014b) "Analysis: Venezuelan Violence Could Leave Maduro Stronger," February 15th.

The Guardian (2014c) "Analysis: Venezuelan Violence Could Leave Maduro Stronger," February 15th.

The Guardian (2014d) "Venezuela's Poor Join Rising Tide of Protests," February 21st.

The Guardian (2014e) "Jailed Lopez Tells His Allies to Keep Fighting," February 22nd.

The Guardian (2014f) "Venezuela Shows Protest Can Also Be a Defence of Privilege," April 10th.

Hart, P. (2014) "Who Is Dying in Venezuela? A Revealing NYT Correction," *FAIR.org*, March 26th, http://fair.org/blog/2014/03/26/who-is-dying-in-venezuela-a-revealing-nyt-correction/

Humphrey, M. and Valverde, E. (2014) "Hope and Fear in Venezuelan Democracy: Violence, Citizen Insecurity, and Competing Neoliberal and Socialist Urban Imaginaries," in Angosto-Ferrandez, L. (ed.) *Democracy, Revolution and Geopolitics in Latin America: Venezuela and the International Politics of Discontent*, London: Routledge.

The Independent (2014a) "Venezuela Face Chaos as Opposition Leader Leopoldo Lopez Surrenders to Authorities," February 18th.

Johnston, J. (2014) "Venezuela: Who Are They and How Did They Die?" *CEPR*, March 12th, http://cepr.net/blogs/the-americas-blog/venezuela-who-are-they-and-how-did-they-die-new

Main, A. and Beeton, D. (2015) "The Latin America WikiLeaks Files," *Jacobin*, September 29th, www.jacobinmag.com/2015/09/latin-america-wikileaks-hugo-chavez-rafael-correa-obama-venezuela-intervention/

McCoy, J. (2014) "Can Venezuela Back Down From the Cliff?" *Al-Jazeera*, March 13th, www.aljazeera.com/indepth/opinion/2014/03/can-venezuela-back-down-from-cli-20143136346997108.html

Miami Herald (2014a) "Thousands Gather in Doral and Across the Globe to Support Anti-government Protests in Venezuela," February 22nd.

Miami Herald (2014b) "The Fight Is Between Nicolas Maduro and the Venezuelan People," February 26th.

Miami Herald (2014c) "Venezuela for Dummies," February 28th.

Miami Herald (2014d) "Should US Cut Venezuelan Oil Imports?" February 26th.

Miami Herald (2014e) "Defiant Opposition Leader Leopoldo Lopez Detained Amid Venezuela Protests," February 18th.

Nagel, J. (2014) "Should Protests End? Polls Suggest So (Updated)," *Caracas Chronicles*, April 7th, http://caracaschronicles.com/2014/04/07/should-protests-end-polls-suggest-so/

Naím, M. (2014) "The Tragedy of Venezuela," *The Atlantic*, February 25th, www.theatlantic.com/international/archive/2014/02/the-tragedy-of-venezuela/284062/

New York Times (2014a) "Rash Repression in Venezuela," February 25th.

New York Times (2014b) "Protesting in Streets of Venezuela, With an Eye on Cuba's Government," March 26th.

New York Times (2014c) "Venezuela Goes Mad," March 11th.

New York Times (2014d) "The Blame Game in Venezuela," March 15th.

New York Times (2014e) "Venezuelan Opposition Chief Surrenders, but not Without a Rally," February 19th.

New York Times (2014f) "Venezuela Accuses Intelligence Officers of Murdering Two," February 27th.

New York Times (2014g) "Venezuela's Opposition Behind Bars," March 26th.

New York Times (2014h) "Slum Dwellers in Caracas Ask, 'What Protests?'" March 1st.

Noticias24 (2014) "Hinterlaces: 87% de los venezolanos está en desacuerdo con las manefestaciones violentas," March 25th, www.noticias24.com/venezuela/noticia/230504/hinterlaces-87-de-los-venezolanos-rechaza-acciones-violentas-en-el-pais/

Pearson, T. and Mallett-Outtrim, R. (2015) "Venezuelan Guarimbas: 11 Things the Media Didn't Tell You," *Venezulanalysis*, February 16th, http://venezuelanalysis.com/analysis/11211

Rosas, D. (2014) "Unasur rechaza actos violentos en Venezuela y se solidariza con el Gobierno," *Correo del Orinoco*, February 15th, www.correodelorinoco.gob.ve/nacionales/unasur-rechaza-actos-violentos-venezuela-y-se-solidariza-gobierno/

Smilde, D. (2014) "Q&A Understanding Venezuela's Protests," *Washington Office on Latin America*, March 7th, www.wola.org/commentary/understanding_venezuela_s_protests

Telesur (2015b) "Venezuelan Victims of Opposition Violence Demand Justice," February 12th, www.telesurtv.net/english/news/Venezuelan-Victims-of-Opposition-Violence-Demand-Justice-20150212-0003.html

The Times (2014a) "Maduro's Misrule," March 12th.

The Times (2014b) "Bazooka Bouts Lead Anti-Maduro Revolt," April 9th.

The Times (2014c) "Venezuela Spies Held Over Protest Killings," February 28th.

The Times (2014d) "Venezuela Spies Held Over Protest Killings," February 28th.

Tinker-Salas, M. (2014) "What Is Happening in Venezuela?" *Truth-out*, March 6th, http://truth-out.org/news/item/22258-what-is-happening-in-venezuela

Tinker-Salas, M. (2015) *Venezuela: What Everyone Needs to Know*, Oxford: Oxford University Press.

Toro, F. (2014a) "The Game Changed in Venezuela Last Night- and the International Media Is Asleep at the Switch," *Caracas Chronicles*, February 20th, http://caracaschronicles.com/2014/02/20/the-game-changed/

Toro, F. (2014b) "Visualize May," *Caracas Chronicles*, February 22nd, http://caracaschronicles.com/2014/02/22/visualize-may/

Washington Post (2014a) "Venezuela Unravels," February 19th.

Washington Post (2014b) "Ignoring Venezuela," March 30th.

Washington Post (2014c) "The Protestors Have Won," March 2nd.

Washington Post (2014d) "Carnival Comes at a Time of Turmoil in Venezuela," February 27th.

White House (2015) "Fact Sheet: Venezuela Executive Order," March 9th, www.whitehouse.gov/the-press-office/2015/03/09/fact-sheet-venezuela-executive-order

Part II

Twenty-seven journalists and academic specialists were interviewed as part of this study. Those interviews constitute the basis of the attempt to answer why the media portrayed the country in the manner it did. In part one we saw the media narrative that dominated was that the *chavistas* had destroyed a once thriving democracy and economy and turned it into a dictatorship and an economic catastrophe. The dissenting opinion that the *chavistas* had improved Venezuela was rarely expressed in the coverage, despite this being supported by the weight of empirical evidence. Why did virtually the entire media present Venezuela in such an overwhelmingly critical manner, so closely following their government and the opposition's lines? We must first look at journalists' backgrounds.

6   Who are the journalists?

Journalists' backgrounds

Journalists worldwide increasingly come from privileged backgrounds. Over half of leading British journalists were privately educated and nearly forty percent are Oxbridge graduates, with seven out of ten attending one of the country's most prestigious universities (Sutton Trust, 2006). In the US, over 92 percent of journalists were college graduates, up from 82 percent in 1992 and 58 percent in 1971. Men outnumber women two to one. Sixty percent of journalists see their profession going the wrong way, with only a third of respondents claiming to have full autonomy over their jobs, compared with nearly two thirds in 1982 (Wilnat and Weaver, 2014).

The reasons for the increasing class homogeneity of journalism are manifold. Most journalism jobs are located in big cities like London or New York. The extremely high costs related to moving to and living in metropolises prohibit those from modest backgrounds following that path, as do rising university fees, meaning many graduates are under intense pressure to immediately earn a high wage. Low pay and insecurity at low levels lead many new journalists to quit. Still more are sacked as newsrooms shed staff (see Chapter 7), yet they are expected to produce more content than ever. Unpaid internships are an increasingly necessary first step to a career in the media, meaning those without financial security will not apply. Furthermore, the informal recruitment process in the industry biases those with personal connections to decision-makers, further privileging those at the top of society (Sutton Trust, 2006).

Journalists coming from this narrowed background tend to have similar political views. Herman (1982: 149) put it succinctly that journalists are,

> Predominantly white middle class people who tend to share the values of the corporate leadership, and they are affected by the fact that

approval, advancement and even job survival depend on an acceptance of certain priorities. The biases at the top are filtered down by long-term penalties and rewards. The mass media top leadership puts into key position individuals who reflect their values.

Journalists coming from elite backgrounds are increasingly distanced from the everyday reality of the population, and are less likely to share the views of the majority and less likely to report on problems affecting the working-class. In more unequal countries like Venezuela, this problem is exacerbated. Furthermore, the rigid, top-down structure of news organizations mean those thinking about career advancement will not "rock the boat" by producing content they know is contrary to the views of the editors, owners and advertisers. Those who do not conform will be passed over for promotion and not have their contracts renewed. As seen in Chapters 1–5, editorials were particularly aggressive towards the Venezuelan government, suggesting editorial staff were highly critical of the Venezuelan government. Thus, the system selects for conformity to the dominant ideology (neoliberalism) and ways of thinking. Former US Federal Communications Commission Chairman Nicholas Johnson described the four stages of conformity and self-censorship in newsrooms:

> A reporter . . . first comes up with an investigative story idea, writes it up and submits it to the editor and is told the story is not going to run. He wonders why, but the next time he is cautious enough to check with the editors first. He is told by the editor that it would be better not to write that story. The third time he thinks of an investigative story idea but doesn't bother the editor with it because he knows it's silly. The fourth time he doesn't even think of the idea anymore.
>
> (Parenti, 1993: 41)

The journalists interviewed for this project were very courteous and generous and were quite open about their work. They were demographically representative, most being male, liberal professionals who came from privileged backgrounds and attended prestigious universities and most reproduced the dominant narrative on Venezuela. A full list of those interviewed is available at the end of the introduction. Journalist 1's background was representative of the cohort:

Journalist 1: Six or seven months after I graduated college I got a job at a newswire. It used to be the real-time news service of some finance companies. I was writing about

the US stock market and other mundane things. Then
I started writing about developing countries and then
came to Venezuela and since then I have been writing
for both my newspaper and the newswire.

However, a small minority of journalists did not share the opinions
of the majority and were highly critical of the coverage. Their backgrounds were different. Matt Kennard was introduced to journalism
through Herman and Chomsky's *Manufacturing Consent*, which, as
discussed in the introduction and Chapter 8, posits that the purpose
of the media is to engineer public consent for elite ideology while Bart
Jones originally came to Venezuela with a Catholic organization that
sent people to live and work with the poor:

Bart Jones: This was in a neighbourhood where there was no running water, no paved streets; most people lived in mud
huts, similar to what Chavez grew up in or in tin shacks.
They were very poor people. It was a great experience as
a journalist because I really got a first-hand view of how
the poor lived in Venezuela and Latin America and why
they were supporting a guy like Chavez. My experience
there was a little bit different to most journalists.

The cornerstone of the support for the *chavistas* has been their social-
democratic and liberal reforms, introducing and expanding free healthcare, education and improving public transport and housing. Yet, liberal
journalists writing in liberal newspapers have been harshly critical of the
government. What explains this discrepancy? One possibility is that,
through editorial control, thoughts of promotion or self-censorship,
journalists produce content that runs contrary to their belief. Philo and
Berry's (2004, 2011) studies of the media coverage of the Israel/Palestine
conflict found that many journalists were sympathetic to the Palestinian
cause but were intimidated into providing Israel with positive coverage.
However, in nearly ten hours of interviews, those journalists reproducing the dominant narrative had nothing positive to say about the country and the social changes of the past two decades. Indeed, when asked
directly what they believed about Venezuela, some were very frank:

Anatoly Kurmanaev: I got here two years ago which you could call
the tail end of this political process of the Bolivarian Revolution. By now the vast majority of
enthusiasm, passion and commitment people
had for the potential of this change to improve

> the country has gone. People are still with the government because it gives them the economic perks to buy things they want rather than actual belief in the idea of socialism. So yeah, it is a pretty depressing place in that sense. Most people are trying to leave the country. It is very difficult; the security situation makes everyone really paranoid and no one really believes the slogans anymore.

The majority of journalists responding to the question gave more "diplomatic" answers, stating that there were serious drawbacks to living there but that was a journalistic goldmine as there were always newsworthy events happening. Therefore, the lack of positive coverage cannot be fully explained due to self-censorship. In fact, Chapter 7 will show that it was actually the dissenting journalists who self-censored, knowing more balanced or positive reporting would not be published. The lack of positive coverage in the press is mirrored by a lack in anything positive to say about the country at all from the journalists interviewed meaning their stories matched their own views on the country.

We should keep in mind that in the US and UK the liberal attitude to Venezuela is very much antagonistic, as it is inside the country. Historically, social democrats in the US and UK have been strongly against social-democratic movements in the global south. For example, the liberal Johnson administration helped to overthrow President Joao Goulart in Brazil in 1964, despite Goulart modeling himself on John F. Kennedy. Meanwhile, British Labour governments have suppressed labour movements all over the world, for example, in Malaysia and Guyana (Blum, 2003). In Venezuela, the liberal AD party is in opposition to the government, thus it common to identify as a liberal and oppose *chavista* reform. Indeed, as seen in Chapter 4, the opposition's last presidential candidate, Henrique Capriles, presented himself as a progressive. Therefore, a phenomenon much more peculiar than purely journalistic self-censorship explains the coverage. One important explanatory variable is the social-political context in which journalists are placed when they go to Venezuela.

Journalists' lack of expertise

The majority of journalists spoken to specifically covered Venezuela for a living. Yet many of them admitted that there were serious holes in their understanding of the social and political situation, especially at first, as can be seen in the following examples,

Interviewer: How familiar are/were you with the social, political and cultural issues of Venezuela?

Girish Gupta: I came *very* ignorant actually. The first year or so I was just trying to learn and get my head round things, both learning journalism and . . . learning about Venezuela, politics, and economics.

Some of the correspondents also began their jobs without speaking Spanish.

Interviewer: Did you speak Spanish before you got here?

Girish Gupta: When I got here my Spanish was non-existent. I just bumbled along and now it is obviously pretty good.

Journalist 1:   (emphasis added)No, I just promised my bosses that I could learn very fast! I used to speak Italian very well so when I got here I did not have trouble reading Spanish. I had trouble with the accents but I would say I was functional *within a few months.*

Thus, many journalists were functionally incapable of speaking Spanish *for months.* Very few people speak English in Venezuela. The country lies behind states such as Oman and Yemen in English proficiency, and fluency is highly correlated with socioeconomic position (Education First, 2015). Journalists are dropped into a political cauldron with little experience, often without even the ability to speak to the bottom 90–95 percent of the population and invariably inhabit the richest, most exclusive areas of Caracas and rarely venture into the hillside slums where over 50 percent of Caracas, and most of the working-class population resides.

Where journalists live

All journalists spoken to lived or stayed in Chacao in Eastern Caracas. As discussed in the introduction, Chacao is the wealthiest municipality in Venezuela, home to 71,000 of the country's richest citizens, to five star hotels and the headquarters of multinational corporations, completely unrepresentative of Venezuela as a whole. It is also one of the strongest bastions of opposition to the *chavista* government. It transpired that there was a relatively close-knit community of ex-pat journalists living and working together.

Journalist 1: Everybody lives fairly close to one another.
Interviewer: Do all the journalists hang out together?
Journalist 1: (emphasis added) Yes and no, I have a couple of journalist friends I hang out with more than others but *I guess it could be seen that way.*
Jim Wyss: I can see the house of the reporter for *The Guardian* from where I am sitting. . . . I think almost everybody is living on the wealthier area because it is really one of the few places that is safe to walk around. Security is a real issue in Venezuela.[1]

Journalists' safety is a serious issue as the *barrios* of large Latin American cities like Caracas are notoriously dangerous. Outsiders are treated with suspicion, particularly foreign journalists, who are often seen as lying enemies. As a result, journalists are understandably discouraged from venturing from the relative safety of Chacao municipality. However, this is a crucial problem if they are cutting themselves off from the 98 percent of poorer Caracas residents who do not live there, especially because they will encounter comparatively few working-class people at work, in their neighbourhoods or in their social circles. *This is particularly important because class is the fundamental fault line along which Venezuelan society is split.* Trying to analyze Venezuelan society without knowledge of or constant contact with the majority of the population is akin to trying to understand a chess game without seeing black's moves, or even knowing about black's pieces. The highly racially and socially segregated geography of Caracas contributes to journalists living and working in a socially constructed bubble.

The bubble

Most of the journalists interviewed confidently asserted that they are largely free to think and write whatever they want about Venezuela. If we accept their assurances, however, we are left with an extremely important question: Why do all these different journalists from all around the world, representing a wide range of news organizations, all have distinctly similar opinions on what is one of the most controversial political topics in the modern world? As shown in Chapters 1–5, the range of opinions of Venezuela could not be wider. Yet there is a much narrower range of opinions shared in the majority of reporting.

Julia Buxton raised a crucial insight in answering this question. Foreign journalists become part of an intermeshed international ex-pat
community of the wealthy middle-class.

Julia Buxton: Overall those networks of circles of influence are interconnected, so if you are a journalist from *El País* or
The Miami Herald, you would feel quite comfortable
sitting down with a journalist from *The Guardian* in
the cocktail lounge of the Hilton Hotel. Those people
would all coincide on their views and perspectives but
those would in turn also be framed by domestic political readerships in those countries.

One *Guardian* journalist I interviewed seemed to corroborate this
view:

Sibylla Brodzinsky: I stayed in Altamira [a neighbourhood of
Chacao]. . . . I checked with colleagues here –
Maria from *Associated Free Press* and Jim Wyss
from *The Miami Herald* – and they helped me
with updating some phone numbers and getting
some new contacts.

Some may be surprised to learn that journalists who write for the
most left-wing major newspaper in the English-speaking West, home
of the far left, is close friends with journalists with people writing
for the most conservative sources in the English-speaking world on
the topic. However, media analysts have argued (Bennett, 2001: 164;
Davies, 2009: 147) the left-wing private media and the right-wing private media have long shared more opinions and interests in common
than they have had disagreements and that they have a propensity to
hunt in packs, spending a great deal of time together and developing a sense of group solidarity and resulting in the phenomenon of
groupthink on many issues. This is particularly the case with foreign
journalists.

Indeed, Brodzinsky had also written for *The Miami Herald*, as well
as the voice of global capitalism, *The Economist*. Francisco Toro has
also written for the left-leaning *Guardian* in addition to the right-
wing *Washington Post* and the extremely conservative *Miami Herald*.
A reader might expect that writing for both extreme ends of the political spectrum to be impossible. However, *on the issue of Venezuela the*

entire Western media gamut is sufficiently narrow as to be traversed by one single voice. There is largely only one opinion expressed. And it is a neoliberal one. While there may be some room for small differences, virtually the entire catalog of news and opinions on Venezuela in the international media is sufficiently similar as to seem plausible that it was written by the same person. The language the Brodzinsky uses – her "colleagues" at *The Herald* –appears to confirm the journalistic solidarity thesis.

In the wake of the Brexit referendum and the Trump presidential victory, there has been a great deal of talk that journalists live in elite bubbles, rarely leaving London or coastal cities like Washington, D.C. or New York, and that this hindered their understanding and reporting. With regards to Venezuela, however, it is one *municipality* of a city that journalists rarely leave. Journalists agreed that the polarization of political opinion between the rich light-skinned middle-class and the poor, dark-skinned working-class and their segregation had a negative effect on reporting, leading to an echo-chamber, particularly for those journalists who are parachuted into the country without a great deal of background knowledge of the situation, stay in expensive hotels, meet one or two prearranged English-speaking contacts and leave soon thereafter. Much of the news on the country comes from this style of journalism, something journalists understood to hinder reporting:

Brian Ellsworth: Definitely, correspondents that rotate a lot, there is a certain echo-chamber that you can get sucked into and a certain outside vision of the way people want to see a country. . . . Yeah, there are people who live in the ex-pat cocoon but I would not describe my life that way.

Francisco Toro: "It is *clearly* a problem. Venezuela is a very polarized society. . . . Obviously when journalists arrive, Caracas is an incredibly dangerous city, even the safe areas are really dangerous and the dangerous areas are absurd. So there is a tendency to cave up in the little eastside bubble in Caracas, where the fancy mansions are and where the English-speaking sources are – this is another thing, it is so nice having a source that speaks English! So the foreign press does get accused of being blinkered in its social scope and having a hard time piercing that bubble. I think that is a fair criticism.

The very high level of crime further dissuaded many from actively looking for another opinion,

Anatoly Kurmanaev: The violence in Venezuela, the security situation makes it difficult for you to just go out there and do objective, broadly sourced reporting you would do in other countries because you just cannot go and walk around the streets. . . . So you are constrained because you are living in that bubble, staying at the Marriott because it is relatively safe, staying in that zone, meeting a couple of economists who everyone else talks to.

Thus, living, working and talking to people mostly within the highly polarized Caracas gives journalists a warped view of the country, a view that closely coincides with the opposition's viewpoint. One interviewee described what it was like staying in Chacao:

Lee Salter: There's an institutionalized pressure that occurs in these news organizations. Correspondents are housed in well-heeled parts of Caracas. *If you ever go there, you cannot mention, in English, that you think the Bolivarian Revolution is anything other than some Nazi Blitzkrieg over Venezuela. If you say anything other than that then they are on you . . .* So there is that social pressure. These people invite you to their garden parties. You want to go for a drink in your local bar or café and if they think you are a supporter of Chavez then you are going to get it in the neck all the time.

In his book about Venezuela, Irish journalist Michael McCaughan (2004: 5) claimed that after mentioning to him that he was going to a Chavez rally, he was physically assaulted by a "literally frothing mouthed" hotel manager. The manager kicked him out the hotel and he *needed an armed police escort* to go to another hotel. He also claimed he saw 8-year-old children at a wealthy private school in East Caracas who were encouraged to chant "death to Chavez" (Ibid: 156–157). Journalists' safety may be at risk if they step outside the established paradigm.

It is a well-established saying that when one is accustomed to privilege, equality feels like oppression. For centuries, the Venezuelan elite have presided over a deeply economically and racially unequal country, controlling the economy, politics, media and civil society. Since 1998, the *chavista* movement has expressly challenged their hegemonic status in all fields with programs aimed at increasing economic, racial, social and cultural equality through social programs, taxes and nationalizations. Therefore, it is an existential threat to the power and status of those in Chacao. In a highly unequal society like Venezuela, increased equality can feel like a "Nazi Blitzkrieg". This is compounded by the actions of the Venezuelan government

The *Chavista* silent treatment

The Venezuelan opposition is very happy to observe the traditional protocols and provide the media with quotes, interviews and references. They are experienced in working with the international media; most of their leaders speak English and share a similar cultural background. Indeed, many were the journalists' classmates; Julio Borges studied at Oxford University, Leopoldo Lopez at Harvard and Henrique Capriles at Columbia. They are quick to respond to emails and telephone calls. In contrast, the *chavistas* come from a different stratum of society and do not prioritize good relations with the international media, who they see as dishonest and engaged in an information war against them. As such, they have effectively shunned them. This reinforces the effect of the polarization, as Toro explained.

Francisco Toro: People in the government will not talk to you; *chavistas* will talk to you but people in the government no. And you need sources and you are living in this socially constructed bubble in the East side of Caracas so that is who you are going to talk to.

This compounds the already problematic reporting, as Ellsworth explained,

Brian Ellsworth: The implicit strategy there is that the questions never get answered. And I think it also has to do with the fact that for quite some time the government decided that the press was an enemy and that there was no value in trying to promote its image in the press, simply because there was no respect for the press . . . it ends up being this vicious circle where you talk less to the press so there is less actual information and rumors just bounce around and no one responds to them, so they just become truths.

Furthermore, in Venezuela, because of the class nature of politics, the traditional elites tend to be dismissive if not hostile to government policies and associate themselves with the opposition. Therefore, the traditional "objective experts" that journalists may turn to in Western societies – university professors, think tanks, business representatives, etc. – have very particular views on each subject. This is true in all countries but particularly the case in unequal Latin American societies where social mobility is very low. As a consequence, it can often seem to a journalist that "everybody" has negative views of the situation in Venezuela. This is because a disproportional amount of Venezuelans that a journalist meets does hold these negative views, because *they are meeting a pre-selected subset of the population that coincides closely with opposition supporters.*

The next chapter deals with the inner workings of how news gets made, and how this shapes the coverage.

Note

1 At the time of the interview, Wyss lived in Bogota, but the quote is illustrative of the small world of journalists in Latin America.

References

Bennett, L. (2001) *News: The Politics of Illusion*, Fourth Edition, London: Longman.

Blum, W. (2003) *Killing Hope: US Military and CIA Interventions Since World War II*, London: Zed Books.

Davies, N. (2009) *Flat Earth News: An Award-winning Reporter Exposes Falsehood, Distortion and Propaganda in the Global Media*, London: Vintage.

Education First (2015) "The English Proficiency Index, 2015," *Education First*, http://media2.ef.com/__/~/media/centralefcom/epi/downloads/full-reports/v5/ef-epi-2015-english.pdf

Herman, E. (1982) *The Real Terror Network: Terrorism in Fact and Propaganda*, Montreal: Black Rose.

McCaughan, M. (2004) *The Battle of Venezuela*, London: Latin American Bureau.

Parenti, M. (1993) *Inverting Reality: The Politics of News Media*, New York: St. Martin's Press.

Philo, G. and Berry, M. (2004) *Bad News From Israel*, London: Pluto.

Philo, G. and Berry, M. (2011) *More Bad News From Israel*, London: Pluto.

Sutton Trust (2006) "The Educational Background of Leading Journalists," June, www.suttontrust.com/public/documents/2Journalists-backgrounds-final-report.pdf

Wilnat, L. and Weaver, D. (2014) *The American Journalist in the Digital Age: Key Findings*, http://news.indiana.edu/releases/iu/2014/05/2013-american-journalist-key-findings.pdf

7 Inside the news factory

Girish Gupta: "The journalism industry is a mess."

The first thing to say about Western coverage of Latin America is that there is not very much of it. This is especially true of tabloid newspapers. Although interest in Venezuela in particular has greatly increased, there is markedly less coverage of Latin America than of Europe and North America. There continues to be almost complete media silence with regards to entire countries such as Paraguay, Ecuador or Bolivia. *Virtually all the information that British and American people receive about Venezuela and South America more generally is created and cultivated by a handful of people.* In 2009, Davies (2009: 104) noted that more than 40 percent of the world's nations have no major newswire staff stationed inside them, and that that figure is rising. Judging by the amount of column inches the continent receives, there is a distinct lack of interest in the West.

There was a distinct feeling among the interviewees that Latin American news mattered little, and there was a shift towards Asia, particularly China, as that is considered the future, geopolitically, and for Western investors. However, due to the connections between Latin America and the US – the region was considered "America's backyard" for a long time – there is more coverage in American newspapers, with *The Miami Herald* providing the most. This is due to the high number of Latinos living in the city that is often referred to as "the capital of Latin America". Therefore, there is still demand for news on Venezuela from some quarters.

Editorial lines and pressures from higher ups

Most of the experts interviewed felt that there was clearly an editorial line. Hudson stated:

Ian Hudson: Unless you have got some sort of theory about the editorial line of the newspaper and the interests that that newspaper serves, you do run into trouble in terms of explaining the stories that get run.

Therefore, the journalists were asked about how the news is made and where the initiative for the stories comes from. There was a mixed response. The ideas for most of the stories they run come from themselves. However, on occasion, they were instructed to write about a particular topic or incident. The journalists were also asked how much pressure they felt they were under from their editors. They initially rejected the idea that they were under any pressure to conform to a certain editorial line, as some academics believed. Furthermore, journalists who reproduced the dominant narrative on Venezuela dismissed the claim that editors censored them. Jim Wyss said:

Jim Wyss: I have never heard anybody in the international press saying they were being restricted in any way.

Yet the dissenting journalists, Jones and Kennard, contradicted this idea.

Bart Jones: (emphasis added) What you might see from [your editors in] New York a little bit more would sometimes be some of the direction too, when it came to the political stuff anyway. *They were very careful to make sure that a certain point of view was strongly in there. . . . I think you definitely had to temper what you were writing. There was a clear sense that Chavez was a threat to democracy and we really need to be talking to these opponents and get that perspective out there.* You know, there was an emphasis put on that.

When told that his colleagues said they do not temper what they write, Jones responded:

Bart Jones: Right, because they are with the anti-Chavez and anti-Maduro line now. So that is acceptable, that is ok for these organizations to write that way.

Kennard claimed he practiced self-censorship in anticipation of editorial censorship:

Matt Kennard: *I just never even pitched stories that I knew would never get in. What you read in my book would just never, ever, in any form, even in news form, get into the FT. And I knew that and I wasn't stupid enough to even pitch it.* I knew it wouldn't even be considered. After I got knocked back from pitching various articles I just stopped.

Interviewer: *So it sounds like it is self-censorship.*

Matt Kennard: Completely. But most people don't realize they are doing it . . . if Simon Romero of *The New York Times* started writing pro-Chavez articles, he'd be out on his ear soon enough.

He also gave specific examples of editorial censorship in favour of state power:

Matt Kennard: At the *FT*, I actually carried on writing as I would. So I put in things like 'US-backed' when describing US-backed dictators, when the convention is to just put 'Russian-backed' or 'Iranian-backed' if they are a bad guy. But I kept doing it because I wanted to test out that *Manufacturing Consent* idea. *And it was explicit. What happens if you put 'US-backed' into a newspaper? Will they take it out? Yes.* And the funny thing is that no one would ever know because the journalists would just never [even] *think* it. It is a form of mind control because everyone thinks they are free. And the best people to write censored articles are people who don't even realize they are performing self-censorship.

In many large organizations, these editors are not in the same building as the journalists. In fact, they are not even on the same continent. For example, Anatoly Kurmanaev said for many pieces he needs the approval of editors in Brazil or New York to write, and it subsequently gets dissected in many stages of editing by people who may never have been to the country. Bart Jones commented on the system: "It is bizarre. Certainly, some editor in London or wherever, what is he going to know about the place?" The multiple levels of editorial bureaucracy a story has to pass through filters the content. Editors are effectively deciding what is news and what the public hears about Venezuela from desks in Brazil, London or the United States. Thus, the worldwide understanding of Venezuela is generated not only by a handful of people, but shaped and edited by administrators who do not live in the country and may have never been there. Editors for large news organizations are likely to have a very particular outlook on the world. Kurmanaev stated:

Anatoly Kurmanaev: You always have editors and they have their ideas, they have a particular way of looking at things which, because they do not live in the country, they do not really see how it really is, they do not really understand it – especially a country like Venezuela which is really hard to get your head around. So, of course, your journalistic output is constrained by your editors' beliefs.

However, the influence of higher-ups on the coverage of Venezuela is not limited to editorial input. Sometimes journalists are essentially instructed to cover an issue by high management and ownership. Jim Wyss confided:

Jim Wyss: Every now and then you will get something from my boss' boss. They will be like 'hey, what do you think about this?' and what that means is 'go out and investigate it'. Or at least prove to them that it is not a story. Every now and then at a cocktail party they will hear something they think is a story and they say 'hey, what do you know about this?' and you have to go and shoot things down. But that is natural with any organization, when your high-up bosses make mild suggestions, you take them very seriously.

The question may be asked whether what an executive or owner hears at a cocktail party about a country with a self-declared socialist government may be accurate and whether rumour and hearsay deserve to be news, or whether their opinions should translate into coverage. Venezuelans at cocktail parties in the United States are likely to be expats with strongly negative views about the country. At least 95 percent of Venezuelans in the US voted for the opposition (*Miami Herald*, 2013). The Miami ex-pat community is disproportionately comprised of wealthy businesspeople with links to the old elite. In contrast, it is unlikely to find a Chavez supporter outside of Venezuela. As Kennard noted:

Matt Kennard: If you meet a Venezuelan in London or Glasgow they're going to be someone who can afford to leave Venezuela and get a plane ticket here to holiday or study. The people from the *barrios* you never hear, just for the prosaic reason that they are just a completely different demographic. When you talk to them, they are a displaced elite. They have had their power taken away from them. They are not going to be happy about it.

The ex-pat community, known to be bastions of hardline conservative anti-*chavista* sentiment also directly contributes to what news and opinions are shared about Venezuela. In addition to flak they give journalists who are not hard enough on the government, according to Wyss,

Jim Wyss: Every now and then editors will hear something that the Venezuelan community or the Miami community is interested in knowing about. [They say] 'Hey, why don't you look into this?'

Therefore, the notorious Miami ex-pat community sometimes dictates the stories and issues that *The Herald* covers. Perhaps this partially explains its reputation as particularly antagonistic with regards to Venezuela and Cuba.

Time and space constraints

Journalists have always worked to a deadline in order that their stories can make it into the newspaper or the television programme. However, with the rise of the Internet, the time pressure has been upped significantly. This is particularly a concern for newswire journalists, whose aim is to beat the competition and make sure their story is picked up before their competitors'. Journalists' professional lives can include hours of boredom followed by minutes of frantic, high-adrenaline action putting together a breaking news story. The pressures are raised due to the fact that newswire journalists are competing over milliseconds to be the first on the wire because people are buying and selling bonds based on what they write. Many journalists agreed that the quality of coverage is often sacrificed to the speed,

Journalist 2:   You have got to be very fast because you are supposed to first in covering anything you are covering. And that speed competes with the depth of the news sometimes.

Jones noted that time pressure made it less likely for journalists to represent the views of ordinary Venezuelans,

Bart Jones: You have got to get the news out right away. And that could be a factor in terms of 'whom can I get a hold of quickly to give me a comment?' Well it is not going to be Juan or Maria over there in the *barrio* because they don't have cell phones. So you can often get a guy like [anti-government pollster] Luis Vicente Leon on the phone very quickly.

This raises the question of how can a journalist really challenge a narrative if they have only a few minutes to write a story. In the era of 24-hour news and Internet journalism, there is a heavy emphasis put on speed. This emphasis has the effect of forcing the journalists to stick to tried and tested narratives and explanations, reproducing what has come before. The importance of being first to print also means that journalists cannot go into detail either, leaving the content both shallow in terms of analysis and similar to previous content. Kennard summed it up:

Matt Kennard: Even if we were inclined [to challenge dominant narratives], there's no time to even do it anyway. If we're on the deadline and we have about five minutes to write a story, we can't go into some extensive analysis of why some term that is used by everyone is wrong.

In addition to this, journalists usually work to a relatively small word limit of only a few hundred words. This further reduces their ability to challenge running narratives. Herman and Chomsky (1988) argued that the effect of concision – having to produce brief pieces of media – has the effect of regurgitating stereotypes and well-trodden narratives. How can somebody cogently argue against a dominant narrative in 400 words of type or 60 seconds of airtime? Concision has the effect of limiting debate, as views that depart from the standard, hegemonic, running narrative cannot be fully articulated in a few words or seconds. In contrast, arguing for the hegemonic worldview is much easier, as the journalist can draw a reservoir of background knowledge and assumptions about the country. Therefore, what we find in the media is many of the same tropes, ideas and facts repeated over and over again.

Journalists operate under a standard capitalistic framework. The question they ask themselves is "will this resonate with readership?" If their stories resonate with readership, they will get clicks, which drives up audience numbers and profits. Today many organizations employ increasingly sophisticated algorithms to track what audiences search for online and to suggest what topics new articles should cover in order to generate the most popular content. Unfortunately, this has led to increasingly alarmist, exaggerated or simply fake stories being published by supposedly trustworthy sources.

Wacky stories, fake news and clickbait

We saw in Chapters 1–5 that there is a great deal of salacious, outlandish stories of dubious veracity about Venezuela in the Western press. Even journalists who produced this content were rather critical of it.

Girish Gupta: A lot of journalists complain to me that clickbait is what they are being asked for. And they have to do it because they are contracted by the company to do it. That is a big problem.

Clickbait is a pejorative term for sensational or provocative stories designed to pique the reader's interest. It is generally considered a cheap trick in the profession. However, in the drive for more views and shares in a competitive marketplace, there was a tendency even for highly-respected news organizations to sex up their stories with catchy titles. Even the BBC, which carries no advertising, told its staff to "emulate *Buzzfeed*" and produce clickbait to generate pageviews (Burrell, 2015). Fake news takes clickbait to another level, often simply inventing inflammatory stories and reporting them as if they were true.

One example of clickbait or fake news is in 2016 when large numbers of supposedly reputable news organizations, including the *Daily Mirror, Fox News* and *The Daily Mail* reported that the economic crisis was so severe that "starving Venezuelans" broke into zoos and ate the animals. There was no evidence for this and was based on a local media report that a horse had died and that "various people" were under investigation. There was no indication whatsoever that starvation or food was connected at all (Mallett-Outrim, 2016).

In contrast, journalists said that stories that were not "sexy" were very hard to sell to editors as worthwhile. This has the effect of shutting off any mainstream reporting of the positive social changes occurring in the country and pigeonholing Venezuela into a wacky country where crazy events happened. Thus, Venezuela becomes a non-serious country run by a crackpot dictator rather than a progressive democratic experiment. This meme produces powerful constraints on introducing alternative perspectives. As a result, no evidence is needed in order to claim Hugo Chavez is a dictator, because it is part of the running narrative. Indeed, some journalists spent an entire article arguing that he was democratically elected, something that should be redundant, like spending an article arguing David Cameron is a Conservative. To describe in an off-hand manner President Barrack Obama as a dictator (as 74 articles in the sample described Chavez) or David Cameron as an authoritarian strongman (as 44 articles did) would be considered a grave breach of journalistic rules. Yet this is the power of the running narrative; ideas that go against it are discarded, ridiculed or attacked because they do not fit the established meme. Davies (2009: 129) describes the danger of the meme:

> The unstated consensus assumption becomes particularly dangerous when it becomes part of a running narrative, so that media outlets are trapped by the story they have told so far, unwilling to allow uncomfortable facts to become part of the story.

For all of this, however, it does not explain in great detail the coverage. Journalists like Owen Jones and Seumas Milne argued against the established narratives and presented the country in a more favourable light. It should be noted Jones and Milne are both well-established journalists in high positions and were very well read. They would therefore have more leeway to argue against the editorial line than many new journalists who have to fear being sacked as newspapers continue to cut staff.

Cuts, cuts and more cuts

Newspapers, television and radio have all suffered sharp drops in audience numbers, leading to a worldwide phenomenon of wholesale cuts in staff (Noam, 2009). Furthermore, the advent of companies such as Google Adsense has enabled corporations to directly target the exact audience they want, bypassing media organizations, leading to reduced advertising rates across all platforms.

Journalists are expected to write more in less time and with fewer resources than ever. Today, there are far more PR staff than journalists (Department of Labour, 2015). This was a common thread in the interviews. There are fewer and fewer foreign correspondents in Latin America. It is also expensive to send a reporter to Venezuela. Flights, hotels, an interpreter, security and a stringer or a fixer are a significant outlay, even for rich news organizations. Smaller news organizations such as regional newspapers rarely spend the money, instead simply mirroring the coverage of the larger newspapers. As news organizations try to trim their payroll and cut costs, they have become increasingly reliant on news wire services and local journalists. The resultant effect on the quality of journalism has taken its toll. One interviewee, Michael Derham said that we are witnessing the "death of the foreign correspondent" before our eyes, with news stories about Venezuela being written from the West by journalists who have never been there.

As a result, "news" appearing in print is often simply regurgitated from press releases and wire services, sometimes rewritten and editorialized to different perspectives but often literally *verbatim* (Davies, 2009: 106–107). This was seen in the sample. For example, *The New York Times* regularly published *Reuters* newswires *verbatim*, whereas *The Daily Telegraph* did the same with both *Reuters* and *AP*. Much of *The Miami Herald's* content came syndicated through The McClatchy Company, which owns more than 30 newspapers in the United States.

The result is far fewer viewpoints on offer. This is a serious threat to the public's right to a wide range of viewpoints on key issues as major newspapers on the opposite side of the political spectrum may have the same news and views. Thus, the Overton Window, the range of political expression in the country, narrows. Cuts in funding have led to fewer and less qualified journalists covering Venezuela. One journalist lamented that their highly knowledgeable editor was sacked and replaced by a succession of half a dozen editors, each cheaper and less capable than the last.

Increasingly, stories about Venezuela are being filed from Brazil or even London or New York. The kind of insight a reporter could have from those locations is debatable. Correspondents who are stationed in Latin America are instructed to cover multiple countries' news from their posts. Two of the interviewees lived in Colombia and only rarely even visited Venezuela. One lived in the United States. The problem with reporting from afar is at least as pressing as the problem of living in the Caracas bubble. How can journalists accurately gauge the public mood if they never interact with the Venezuelan public? What news can journalists report on other than repeating statements from officials or copying something they read on the newswire? Jim Wyss of *The Miami Herald* covered the entire Andean region (including Venezuela) from Colombia, and agreed this hampered his reporting:

Jim Wyss: *Part of the problem is that I am the only person [for the Latino newspaper Miami Herald] in South America. I have my hands quite full between Colombia, Venezuela and Ecuador but it does happen every now and again that something interesting will be happening elsewhere, and I just cannot rationalize it.*

Interviewer: I thought *The Miami Herald* had a very high Latino readership and you are the only one in South America?

Jim Wyss: (emphasis added) Well, it does, in theory. *But with years of budget cuts the paper is about half the size it was when I first started there in 2005. There are three reporters on the world desk: two of them are reporting from Miami; one covers Cuba and Brazil from Miami; the other one covers mainly Haiti and the other parts of the Caribbean. But in terms of in the field, I am it right now. . . . When you talk about full-time newspaper correspondents in Latin America you are talking about The Washington Post, The Wall Street Journal, The New York Times, The Miami Herald . . . and that is it as far as I know.*

Therefore, there are four correspondents for all of Latin America for the entirety of the American press. The death of the foreign correspondent is an accurate metaphor. Even *The Miami Herald*, a newspaper that positions itself as being the voice of the Latino community in the United States, has only one correspondent in South America. Wyss is paid to cover three countries himself, keeping him occupied. Thus, for *The Miami Herald*, news simply does not occur in a number of other South American countries. *In terms of foreign correspondents, Wyss said for major English-language newspapers, only The New York Times has one in Venezuela. There are no full-time correspondents stationed in Venezuela for any British news source. It follows that, for the entirety of the Western English-language press, there is one full-time correspondent in Venezuela.* Consequently, there is a lack of understanding of the country.

Journalists are either parachuted into the country to cover important events without any background of its politics or culture, or simply
cover it from afar. Davies (2009: 100) describes the effect of this style
of journalism:

> This tends to produce a consensus – and conservative – account of
> the world: reporters are flown out from their home bases at a few
> hours' notice and arrive in today's trouble spot with nothing but
> their preconceptions to guide them; then they plug in to a handful
> of obvious sources, usually including their own embassy, to have
> those preconceptions reinforced by official sources.

As we will see, news organizations therefore are highly reliant on
news wires and local stringers. However, this comes with its own
problems.

Reliance on newswires and stringers

In an attempt to save money, newspapers worldwide have reduced
the amount of original content they create by sacking journalists, correspondents and editors, outsourcing their work to stringers or simply repeating the information from newswires such as *Bloomberg* and
Reuters. Sixty percent of British broadsheet news stories consisted
partially or wholly of wire services or PR material, although only one
percent admitted their source (Davies, 2009: 52–53). In terms of the
objectivity and accuracy of the content, this has serious consequences.
International news agencies are fundamentally linked to the international business class and powerful Western interests (Boyd-Barrett,
1980), whose interests are diametrically opposed to the stated aims of
the Bolivarian Revolution.

Inside these news organizations, journalists are not free to write
about what they want. Mirroring the trend other forms of media,
there has been a continued stripping down of staff numbers, the journalists increasingly having to cover only what sells and appeals to their
clients: international business. The primary audience for newswires
such as *Bloomberg* is traders, with the second buyers being broadsheet
newspapers, which cater to upper-middle class audiences. Therefore,
the imperative is to deliver content that resonates with these groups.
This audience is hardly likely to be in favour of governments redistrib-
uting wealth and power downwards, as the Venezuelan government
proposes.

Journalists who fit in well with the culture at such a neoliberal organization are distinctly likely to hold anti-Venezuelan government sentiments. Indeed, during the interviews, the newswire journalists held the strongest anti-government opinions, or were at least the most frank about it. Newswires hold enormous influence in the way in which foreign affairs are framed, due to the worldwide reliance on their content. Virtually everything that appears on a newswire will be picked up and reproduced somewhere, often in dozens, if not hundreds of publications. As a result, content aimed at Wall Street traders, hardly a representative group, is reproduced, often *verbatim*, around the world for mass consumption.

There has been just as pronounced a tendency to outsource news reporting to cheaper, locally-based stringers. One example of this in the cohort was Journalist 2, who worked for both *El Universal* and *El Nacional* before joining an international newswire. But as we saw in Chapters 2 and 4, the Venezuelan media landscape is highly partisan, with the large majority of the major media (including *El Universal* and *El Nacional*) strongly opposed to the government, planning, carrying out, and supporting a number of violent coup attempts, for example in 2002 (see Chapter 2). Journalists working for the traditional news media and fluent in English are overwhelmingly likely to hold highly negative views of the government and recent developments in society, given their class background and the editorial positions the Venezuelan media has taken. Local journalists who support the government are simply not hired. As a result, radical, anti-government activists who were involved in multiple attempts overthrowing their government are now charged with providing accurate, fair and unbiased news about Venezuela and their message is amplified to an enormous extent through the practice of outsourcing reporting to them. They are given a veneer of credibility by their association with the country's largest publications. However, it leads to a situation where it is increasingly difficult to differentiate between the Venezuelan and the international media.

The interconnectedness of the Venezuelan and international media

There exists an extremely close relationship between the local media and the international press in Venezuela. Coupled with journalists' own backgrounds and pre-existing biases and the fact that they live in highly segregated affluent communities, this has led to a situation where newsroom culture is extremely hostile to the *chavista* project.

Journalists in Venezuela simultaneously see themselves as impartial technocrats and as ideological foot soldiers in a war against the tyrannical government, as Bart Jones explained,

Bart Jones: There was definitely an atmosphere of 'Chavez is a bad guy', you know? And we need to fully present and almost take the side of the 'resistance', the 'dissidents', or whatever you want to call them. They would *actually use* those terms.

Julia Buxton highlighted how the international press is intricately intertwined with the traditional Venezuelan media through personal, political and professional relations:

Julia Buxton: I do not think that the Venezuelan media and the international media are separable. There are contacts, networks, family and alumni links and business relationships between people in Venezuela and people in the US media so it is absolutely no surprise to me that there would be any overlap between these people. Another issue is that journalists are very lazy. It is very easy to just cut and paste that you have already seen in the media. Rather than having investigative journalism, what we have instead is a recycling of the material. If your newspaper's previous position is to ally itself with the opposition, then it is in your interest to cut and paste or follow the same line as what is being pursued in the US and the UK media. But these people are all interconnected; they are not separate media outlets who happen to coincide, these people are closely related.

All seven newspapers from both countries in this study consistently took editorial positions strongly against the Venezuelan government. None sided with the majority of Venezuelans. As we saw in Chapter 6, journalists live in a bubble of privilege where they spend an inordinate amount of time with members of the Venezuelan elite. New journalists arrive and are socialized into the opposition camp and are immersed into a strongly anti-government culture. They also spend a good deal of their job conversing and working with traditional local journalists, some of whom were leaders in numerous attempts to overthrow the government. Journalists confirmed they had close contact with their local colleagues. However, those spoken to saw this as an advantage.

Brian Ellsworth: I became very close friends with a lot of them and I think it is hugely beneficial to the correspondent because there is a natural, symbiotic relationship there with local reporters. They cover things in more detail than the foreign reporters do so they can help you get ahead on things. And in the other direction, foreign correspondents frequently come into town and say 'I need someone to help me with this' and I say 'go talk to so-and-so' so you can send jobs to people and if they need information from out of the country we can use our own networks to get that sometimes.

Here we can see how personal and professional contacts grow. Foreign reporters are sent to work closely with local journalists, whom they believe to be neutral professionals. This is another strand to the way in which the journalistic bubble is created and maintained. Most international journalists do not see this connection as problematic because they consider their local comrades to be impartial professionals under attack from an authoritarian government.

Much of the content in the international press is actually written by local Venezuelan journalists. In this sense, it can be said that there is little difference between the internal Venezuelan media and the international media. *The Venezuelan media is the international media and vice versa.* All the major international news organizations and most newspapers have ex-opposition Venezuelan journalists on their staff. For instance, *The Guardian* and the BBC have employed Virginia López-Glass, a local journalist hostile to the government, while Emilia Díaz-Struck, who writes for *The Washington Post*, also wrote for *El Nacional* and *El Universal*: two newspapers that helped overthrow the government in 2002. She also co-founded the news site *Armando. info*, which runs stories with one thing in common: an aversion to the Venezuelan government. Of his colleagues, Bart Jones said:

Bart Jones: Some of them were outright government haters. One of them said it to me once, 'we have got to get rid of this guy.' I think there is a problem in such a heated political environment with people trying to maintain their professional objectivity.

Thus, many journalists working for Western media see themselves as anti-government activists.

But even without Venezuelans writing the content themselves, the content of the traditional private Venezuelan media finds its way into the international media. Journalists are under significant time pressure, and there is a tendency to simply repeat uncritically what they are hearing in the local media. Jones confirmed Buxton's claim about cutting and pasting from local sources:

Bart Jones: We would all definitely read those local papers. That would be your first duty of the day, to see what they had. And they could even directly take from it and make a story out of it. '*El Nacional* reported blah blah blah,' you know? Obviously the local media down there was totally anti-Chavez . . . they were not just anti-Chavez but they were trying to overthrow him. So if you are an international journalist and you are relying on those publications for your information it is a little bit problematic. Especially if you are not even going to do your own reporting and you are just going to take what they say and turn it into a story.

In this fashion, opposition propaganda is amplified onto the world stage, often verbatim, by the Western media. Venezuelan journalists and academics that subscribe to the authoritarian government theme are given a platform in the international media. Those who do not share this viewpoint are ignored.

Intellectuals who have left the country and gone to the West are given credence by the fact they are from Venezuela. However, they very often represent a particular set of interests related to those at the top of society. Prominent opposition figures are awarded the opportunity to write for influential newspapers and magazines. One example of this is Moises Naím, who was former Minister of Trade and Industry under President Carlos Andres Perez. He was one of the key figures behind Venezuela's neoliberal package, which plunged the country into poverty. He was also a major government figure during the *Caracazo*, a government-ordered massacre of the civilian population and the worst massacre in modern Venezuelan history (see Chapter 1). Naím was appointed Executive Director of the World Bank and is one of the key intellectuals behind neoliberal globalization. His views appear all over the world in publications like *Le Monde* (France), *El País* (Spain), *TIME Magazine* (USA), *La Repubblica* (Italy), *The*

Financial Times (UK) and *Berliner Zeitung* (Germany). Despite his background as an opposition politician and being in charge of the economy during the worst economic collapses and massacres in Venezuelan history, Naím is presented as a politically neutral expert rather than an opinionated actor. One of Venezuela's most prominent and strident opposition bloggers, Francisco Toro, was also contracted to produce columns about the country for *The New York Times* and *Washington Post*.

In contrast, pro-government journalists in Venezuela are not asked to help with stories for the foreign press and academics sympathetic to the *chavistas* are rarely contacted for quotes on current events, let alone asked to write articles for establishment publications. As Derham said when asked if he is ever contacted by the media, "Press interest? Absolutely not. I don't think my opinions would fit in with what they want to broadcast." Other academics, such as Kevin Young, found the idea of being contacted for his opinions so unlikely as to be laughable. It transpired that some academics that did not toe the editorial line of the press had, in their own words, been "blacklisted" from the mainstream Western media, a "really common" occurrence for academics who do not repeat the official line, according to Buxton. She explained:

Julia Buxton: Some of these opinion formers around Venezuela are connected to things like the Carnegie Foundation, Heritage Foundation and the Brookings Institute – the usual think tanks. These are populated by Venezuelans who are absolutely antithetical to what happened in 1998 and are recalcitrant in their opposition, but they have the access to the think tanks to be able to articulate that, which is absolutely not the case for people from the pro-government side.

The Brookings Institute, funded indirectly through the US Government and directly by some of the largest banks and corporations in the world, sponsors or prints much of the most anti-Venelzuan government intellectuals, such as Javier Corrales and Michael Penfold, while The Heritage Foundation publishes reports categorizing Venezuela as a "terrorist state" (Walser, 2010). In this way, the anti-government position is boosted by a network of think tanks.

The next part deals with geopolitical explanations for the nature of the reporting.

References

Boyd-Barrett, O. (1980) *The International News Agencies*, London: Constable.

Burrell, I. (2015) "BBC Told to Emulate Buzzfeed by Producing 'Informal' Short Videos Where Reporter Acts as a 'Friend,'" *The Independent*, November 5th, www.independent.co.uk/news/media/bbc-told-to-emulate-buzzfeed-by-producing-informal-short-videos-where-reporter-acts-as-a-friend-a6723216.html

Davies, N. (2009) *Flat Earth News: An Award-winning Reporter Exposes Falsehood, Distortion and Propaganda in the Global Media*, London: Vintage.

Department of Labour (2015) "Occupational Employment Statistics," May, www.bls.gov/oes/#data

Herman, E. and Chomsky, N. (1988) *Manufacturing Consent: The Political Economy of the Mass Media*, New York: Pantheon.

Mallett-Outrim, R. (2016) "How the Western Media Created a Desperate Gang of Venezuelan Horse Eaters," *Venezuelanalysis*, https://venezuelanalysis.com/analysis/12181

Miami Herald (2013) "In South Florida, Venezuelans React to Hugo Chavez's Death," March 5th.

Noam, E. (2009) *Media Ownership and Concentration in America*, Oxford: Oxford University Press.

Walser, R. (2010) "State Sponsors of Terrorism: Time to Add Venezuela to the List," *The Hertiage Foundation*, January 20th, www.heritage.org/research/reports/2010/01/state-sponsors-of-terrorism-time-to-add-venezuela-to-the-list

8   Geopolitics and the propaganda model

The previous chapters demonstrated the reasons for why supposedly objective, unbiased Western reporting of Venezuela so closely mirrors the local opposition parties' propaganda. It is now time to explore why the media closely followed their governments' lines. As shown in Chapters 1–5, the spectrum of political opinions on every topic on Venezuela is extremely wide, ranging from it being a shining example to follow, a tonic to the 21st-century neoliberal malaise (Brouwer, 2011) to a compulsively anti-American Marxist-Leninist terror-state (Walser, 2010). With such a vast array of serious opinions on the topic, it would be possible to have a very open and wide-ranging debate about the country in the media.

But Chapters 1–5 showed that the spectrum of opinions offered by the media was extremely narrow, and largely limited to the critical extreme of opinion, with the newspapers presenting the country much more similarly to the official line of the US government than to the empirical data from the likes of the UN, or even reports the US government had paid for, let alone to the views of the majority of the Venezuelan public.

Geopolitics

Crucial in understanding why such a proscribed, negative range of views was offered, was the positions of the US and, to a lesser extent, the UK governments. Bush's Defense Secretary Donald Rumsfeld labeled Chavez a new Hitler, and President Obama declared a state of emergency in the US because of the "extraordinary threat" posed by Venezuela. Successive US administrations have also spent nearly 20 years trying to overthrow the *chavista* governments and to install pliant governments like those of Carlos Andres Perez and Rafael Caldera. Britain, having accepted its role of junior partner in the "special relationship" followed the US line.

In general, a country's particular media coverage of Venezuela tends to closely correlate to their government's official position. While the newspapers of the United States and United Kingdom have taken antagonistic stances towards the Venezuelan government, Russian state-funded media network *RT* has maintained a sympathetic position towards it (as we saw in Chapter 5). This was an essential detail, according to Ellner:

Steve Ellner: That is what the media is reflecting: the US official position. And it has been that way all along . . . when it comes to foreign policy there is a line. And that line is decided upon from above and passed on to the reporter. So when it comes to hotspots like Venezuela, where there is so much at stake from an ideological viewpoint, even more so. It is as monolithic as you can get.

Therefore, the media do not focus upon the positive societal changes impacting on Venezuela and concentrate on negative stories that place the country in a bad light. Furthermore, there is a constant stream of criticism of the country from Western government officials that the media are expected to cover. This leads to a situation where negative stories about the country are abundant and positive stories are systematically rejected. This tells us a great deal about our media, as Kevin Young explained:

Kevin Young: Most of the coverage of Venezuela tells us far more about the deeply ingrained biased of the US and UK media themselves than about Venezuela. Pretty much everything that does not fit with the official US government narrative is excluded from coverage. So we hear virtually nothing about the positive improvements in social policy in Venezuela over the past 15 years, reductions in poverty, substantial reductions in inequality as well, different programs that exist like the promotion of communal councils, the missions, the efforts to expand healthcare and education. All of those things are systematically omitted from coverage.

As dealt with in the introduction, the United States, and, to a lesser extent, Great Britain have historically opposed progressive or left-wing movements in Latin America, attacking or overthrowing a great number of Latin American governments opposed to their interests, such as the Goulart administration in Brazil, Salvador Allende in Chile, or the Sandinistas in Nicaragua (Blum, 2003) and supporting reactionary dictatorships like General Banzer's Bolivia or General Stroessner's Paraguay. In each case, the US media took the same line as Washington (Parenti, 1993; Herman and Chomsky, 1988).

As discussed in the introduction, Venezuela was the first of a new wave of Latin American countries to elect progressive parties that openly questioned the logic of the "Washington Consensus" – the belief that neoliberalism was the best way to organize society – and to champion the idea of "21st-century socialism". Thanks in large part to Chavez's leadership, South America as a whole has experienced a profound geopolitical shift, moving away from being firmly under the influence of the US and creating a new, independent domestic and foreign policy while creating a raft of new international institutions designed to replace the old, US-dominated ones such as the OAS. According to Bhatt, this made the country the epicentre of a new Latin American independence movement extricating itself from US control. Other countries following this path, such as Bolivia and Ecuador have been presented similarly negatively in the Western press (Lupien, 2013; Young, 2013).

The logic of allowing foreign (usually Western) corporations to enjoy near unlimited power in and reap huge profits from South America has been challenged in many places, with some Western companies having been nationalized. Furthermore, Venezuela also resurrected the power of OPEC in 1999, with the first OPEC summit in 25 years taking place in Caracas in 2000. Oil prices rose from $9 per barrel in 1999 to $140 in 2008 (NASDAQ, 2017). This meant that oil-consuming nations (like the US) were paying hundreds of billions of dollars more per year for their oil.

Reacting to this, the US government organized or supported multiple and continuous attempts at regime change (see Chapters 2 and 5), with leaked documents showing the goal of the government to "divide" and "penetrate" *chavismo* (Beeton et al., 2015). Weisbrot (2014) calculated the government has spent hundreds of millions of dollars trying to destroy the virus. However, the *chavistas'* new ideas in democracy have inspired political movements around the world, including in Europe, where Syriza (Greece) and PODEMOS (Spain) have close links with them. In the UK, many of the key figures of the Labour Party, such as John McDonnell, have close links with the Venezuelan government, and Jeremy Corbyn outlined a plan to bring 21st century socialism to the country. Thus, the virus that began in Venezuela is threatening to spread around the world.

Due to the close relationship between the media and government, this has had its effect on the output of newspapers and general opinion on Venezuela. This was a common cause brought up in explanation for the decidedly negative coverage, as the following quotes highlight,

Keane Bhatt: The documentary record is so rich in terms of constant efforts at destabilization and overthrow through the coup in 2002, through the NED, through USAID, through groups that were the recipients in massive amounts of US aid and training who were involved in the coup and were receiving US money afterwards and then who went on to encourage all kinds of destabilizing campaigns against the Venezuelan government including this most recent violence [the *guarimbas*]. All that stuff is, to an outside observer, so plain and so easy to discover, and [so is] the fact that the US media is so committed to omitting almost every single report, framing it as an allegation Venezuela makes of meddling, without ever providing more than a 'he said she said' allegation and denial. They portray it as a kind of lunatic fringe using this as a pretext for avoiding their own internal problems."

Michael Derham: Venezuela is under attack from the United States, and has been since 1999. It has never let up. It is a media and press attack, an economic attack.

Here Derham raises the idea that the media acts as a vehicle for furthering government foreign policy, a notion at the heart of the Propaganda Model.

The Propaganda Model

As explored in the introduction, Herman and Chomsky's (1988) Propaganda Model posits that news is systematically distorted through a series of five filters to reflect the interests of state and corporate power. These filters are elite ownership of the media, reliance on corporate advertisers as a primary revenue stream, the custom of relying on official sources to shape the coverage, flak and an anti-socialist or anti-communist ideology.

Many of the interviewees highlighted the importance of these five filters in explaining the negative coverage of the country. Indeed, Salter argued that the first filter alone would prove a barrier to any positive coverage of Venezuela:

Lee Salter: *It is incontestable. There is no evidence at all to the contrary to the fact that all of the commercial newspapers in this country are owned by neoliberal businessmen – Richard Desmond, Rupert Murdoch, the Barclay brothers, Alexander Lebedev. They cannot allow an alternative to the system that they both benefit from and ideologically believe to be best, to survive. They can't allow it. . . . Murdoch and all of the British newspaper proprietors are neoliberals and they will give no positive coverage of any left-wing movement anywhere in the world that looks like it is going to succeed. . . .* So those ownership structures tell us a hell of a lot about the paradigms within which facts about the world exist and the selection of those case studies to look at. Hence not one article that says anything positive about the Bolivarian Missions or CELAC or anything but lots that ridicule and disparage it.

Chapter 7 showed how journalists agreed that pressure from ownership, editors and higher-ups affected the coverage and explored how newspapers are under ever increasing financial pressure and are having to constantly cut staff. Fighting for survival, newspapers operating under a standard, advertising-based model simply cannot consistently take editorial positions against those of their advertisers, as they will leave and advertise somewhere else, leading to a terminal reduction in revenues. This situation has effectively given advertisers a veto over political content. Large corporate advertisers are hardly likely to want positive coverage of a government that expropriates businesses or raises taxes on the wealthy.

Journalists are also highly reliant on sources that effectively subsidize them with free content. It is therefore vital not to lose contacts, particularly officials, by reporting in a manner that would upset them. The consequence is a parroting of official lines. A Venezuelan example of uncritical regurgitation of official propaganda is former Congressman Connie Mack IV. Representing the right wing of the Republican Party, and with links to the infamous Cuban ex-pat community, Mack took an extremely hostile position to Venezuela, frequently making claims of dubious validity. However, his status as an official source and his habit for providing extremely quotable opinions meant newspapers frequently quoted his outbursts uncritically. *The Guardian* (2007) used Mack's outburst that Iranian President Mahmoud Ahmadinejad "recognizes that is he can get a foothold in Latin America, he can continue to spread his hatred for the United States" to construct a news story that portrayed Venezuela in a negative light. The notion that Venezuela was helping Iran to conquer South America was not challenged.

Thus, there exists a lack of balance within the stories emanating from Venezuela, where the rather extreme positions of the US government are rarely strongly challenged by the journalists themselves, due, in part to journalistic convention. Davies (2009: 113–114) has argued that this principle leads to "a political and moral consensus which tends to reflect the values only of the most powerful groups in the surrounding society" while Bennett (2001: 182) remarks that "the most important biases in the news occur not when journalists abandon their professional standards but when they cling most responsibly to them".

In contrast, ideas that go against the conventional narrative on Venezuela are challenged, and reporting in such a way threatens a journalist's vital access to government figures, as economist and columnist Dan Beeton described:

Dan Beeton: (emphasis added) A big part of what the media is concerned about is access. *The way things are framed is the US government view, the State Department view of things is the framework in which everything is reported. Anything that goes against that is the outlier and so that is what has to be fact-checked, that is what has to be challenged.* Even when you are writing op-eds you can just make things up! If you are *Associated Press*, certainly if you are *Fox News*, any number of commentators on television and people writing op-eds against Venezuela can basically say whatever they want and won't get fact checked. But if you are saying something that challenges that narrative like we have had experience of again and again talking about the decline in poverty and other positive economic factors after the Chavez government gained control of the oil sector then you get challenged: 'What is your source for this?' 'Where does this come from?' Even though these are basic facts that are accepted by the World Bank, the IMF, the UN and so on. That is the framework.

Thus, the default understanding of Venezuela (and any foreign country) is that of the US government. Content that agrees with this understanding is seen as unbiased whereas content challenging it is controversial.

As discussed in Chapter 6, journalists inside Venezuela live in socially constructed bubbles, living and working in the richest municipality and are unlikely to interact with many people who openly hold views sympathetic to the government, a majority view in the country during the period. The result is an echo chamber effect where the large majority of people journalists meets and talks to hold strongly negative opinions about the state of the country, which translates into overly negative coverage in the media. Many of the non-government sources of authority, such as judges, the civil service, business leaders, journalists and academics came from the sectors of wealth and privilege in Venezuela identified with the *ancien regime*.

Outside of Venezuela, the pool of experts is partially populated by ex-pats who are critical of the government. The cost of a flight to Europe or the USA ($700) equated to more than a year's salary for most of the population in 1998 (CEPALSTAT, 2016a), effectively meaning only the rich have the opportunity to emigrate to the West. Moreover, academics and intellectuals with progressive outlooks who did live in the West are more likely to have gone back to Venezuela to take up positions inside the country to fill the dearth of qualified intellectuals sympathetic to the government. Going the other way are a large group of wealthy citizens who have decided to leave the country due to the political and economic changes. Many have ended up in Miami and other US cities, others in Spain, but some have also come to Great Britain. The result is that an unusually large majority of ex-pats are against the changes that have taken place and stand against everything that the government claims to stand for. At least 95 percent of ex-pats in the US voted for the opposition (*Miami Herald*, 2013). This provides a similar echo chamber effect for journalists in the West. As Bart Jones said, "one point I think is really problematic for the perception of Venezuela in the West is that every Venezuelan we meet is going to be middle-class [anti-government]".

In Venezuela the sources filter is doubly important because, as we have seen, the Venezuelan government does not bother to cultivate good relations with the foreign media. Their policy is effectively to shun them, making it clear they do not wish to speak to them very often. Journalists do not have to worry about the repercussions of criticizing the government or reporting something in a way contrary to the wishes of Venezuelan officials. They will not lose their access to

Venezuelan officials because they never had any. Therefore, the sourcing filter is doubly important when it comes to Venezuela, as journalists turn almost exclusively to sources critical of the government for quotes. The interviewees confirmed this. For example, Girish Gupta noted:

Girish Gupta: (emphasis added) In Venezuela it is near impossible to talk to government officials. *But there are sources in other sectors, people in opposition, it is not just people in government who know things.*

Other journalists noted that they wanted to contact Venezuelan government sources to provide more balanced reporting, but could not.

Flak is a particularly important factor in the coverage of Venezuela because of the extremes of opinion. As Brian Ellsworth said, "Venezuela became this hysterical obsession for people of all different political orientations." Miguel Tinker-Salas, a progressive Venezuelan professor at Pomona College, California, was visited by the FBI who looked into his past, questioning his immigration status and his contact with the Venezuelan government. In 2017, after reporting on anti-government protests, American journalists Abby Martin and Michael Prysner were the subjects of a viral fake news twitter campaign that claimed they were informants gathering information on the protests for the secret police. They were subject to dozens of death threats, and there was a campaign in Venezuela, including among high-profile opposition academics and journalists, to find and lynch them on the basis of these accusations (Gosztola, 2017).

Wyss confided that he did receive angry feedback that steered coverage:

Jim Wyss: (emphasis added) I hear from grumpy readers when they feel I am not being hard enough on Venezuela. I never get any pressure from anybody except from some radical readers who see everything through the prism of Cuba so *if you are not hammering Maduro hard enough you tend to get emails.*

Although, he did note that he tended to ignore them as they were usually in all caps and had a lot of misspellings. Beeton faced considerable pressure from the system:

Dan Beeton: That is the framework. If you are a reporter and you write something that is not considered negative enough against the Venezuelan government then you will get flak. There is push back, maybe from the US government, but there are any number of right-wing think tanks, Venezuelan exiles have their own organizations and lobbies and their champions in the US Congress. . . . We have been challenged repeatedly and questioned any time we say something about it – whether we get funding from the Venezuelan government. There is this assumption that if anyone is saying anything that goes against the conventional wisdom that they must be in the pockets of the Venezuelan government.

With regards to Venezuela, it is clear that the Propaganda Model holds. Yet the five filters cannot fully explain why the country is presented so poorly. One last explanatory variable is the cultural pressure exerted on journalists.

Cultural factors

Despite the geopolitical history of the situation, which the interviewees were aware of, those reproducing the dominant narrative on Venezuela treated the notion of Western government or media nefariousness as ridiculous. Journalists interviewed were aware that large sections of the public held negative views about them, but treated these views as strange, at best, and risible, at worst. Anatoly Kurmanaev described the Venezuelan government as "paranoid" to believe the media could be trying to overthrow it, and that the President will "rant" and,

Anatoly Kurmanaev: Go on television and accuse them [the media] of trying to foment a coup and trying to sabotage the country and being in the pay of the CIA, *etc.* But that is just words, smoke and mirrors. . . . It is pretty much a one-party state . . . and as a reporter for a Western outlet, you are seen as an enemy by a significant chunk of the population; you are seen as part of a system that is trying to overthrow this government.

He said that the government say to him they "have to blame things on someone so don't get upset if once in a while we go on television and rave against you for a bit" and that "it is just part of a game". Thus, the idea the media have any ulterior motives is considered absurd.

This benevolent Westerner theme extends even to the US government, whose record in overthrowing Latin American governments has been detailed above. In his book about contemporary Brazil, Larry Rohter, who wrote many articles on Venezuela for *The New York Times*, noted that some Brazilian intellectuals actually believe that the US government has held Brazilian development back by using its resources for itself. He goes on to state "this is not a fringe school of thought but one expressed by respected historians . . . and taught in universities" (2010: 229). The wording suggests Rohter does not think his audience would believe such a concept could be a widespread belief – "this is *not* a fringe school of thought" or a credible one – "but one expressed by respected historians". In other words, Rohter is telling his audience "seriously, people *actually* believe this".

Thus, many journalists consider much of the criticism of their profession and the American government to be ludicrous and virtually beneath consideration. This came out in the reporting, where, as we saw in Chapters 2 and 5, points of view critiquing the US government or those differing from neoliberalism were ignored or treated as "absurd" and "outlandish" conspiracy theories.

Yet Chapters 2 and 5 demonstrated how the local and international media supported the 2002 coup and the 2014 *guarimbas*, the attempt to unconstitutionally oust the government, while Washington supported the overthrow of the Brazilian government in 1964 and spied on President Dilma Rousseff during the 2010s. Furthermore, many studies (Lupien, 2013; Young, 2013; Delacour, 2005) have highlighted the media's strong bias in Venezuela. To explain why journalists continue to believe the opposite we must study the cultural dynamic.

Herman and Chomsky argued this cultural dynamic is a strong factor in shaping news, stating that the manufacture of consent is not normally accomplished through crude editorial intervention but by,

> The pre-selection of right-thinking people, internalized preconceptions, and the adaptation of personnel to the constraints of ownership, organization, market, and political power. Censorship is largely self-censorship, by reporters and commentators who adjust to the realities of source and media organizational requirements, and by people at higher levels within media organizations who are chosen to implement, and have usually internalized, the constraints imposed by proprietary and other market and governmental centers of power.

> (2002: Preface)

As we saw in Chapter 6, journalists live in the most exclusive parts of a highly segregated Caracas. The country is split between the poor working-class that largely support the government and the elites who strongly oppose it. Journalists live, work and spend the great deal of their time in walled off citadels of privilege, gated communities with armed guards, and do not interact with a great number of government supporters. Furthermore, the large majority of their contacts and colleagues at work strongly oppose the government, leading to an overwhelmingly anti-government atmosphere milieu. Journalists who come to Caracas are welcomed by the opposition, who look, dress and speak like they do, often having attended the same universities. In contrast, they are treated with suspicion or hostility by the *chavistas*, who see them as the enemy. As a consequence, there is a powerful hegemony of thought in the newsroom that acts as a strong deterrent from taking alternative positions. Matt Kennard, who was not a "right-thinking" employee, stated that the cultural pressure was not a conscious power acting upon his colleagues:

Matt Kennard: Nobody is thinking, 'I want to be a warmonger and support neoliberal economics to further my career.' It doesn't work like that. But if everyone else is thinking it around you, it is very hard to go into work every day and be at odds with everyone. You'd seem like a weirdo . . . that's the beauty of the system. It is not like the Soviet system. It is not like you will be put in jail. You just won't rise. And that's why no one ever thinks these things. It is just implicit in what you do.

He went on to say:

Matt Kennard: It's not because they are stupid. Some of the smartest columnists at the *Financial Times* would never think of doing it. It is a form of mind control, of mind training. . . . There's a complete lack of self-criticism. And there's a reason for that: people like to think they are independent journalists that do their trade without fear or favour – all this bullshit you're taught at journalism school.

One method that tried to get the journalists to critically evaluate the coverage was to present them with the example of *RT*, which portrayed the country and the government greatly more positively than did any newspaper in the study. It was explained that it might be partly down to the geopolitical positions of Russia, Great Britain and the US. One journalist was asked how they would explain this conspicuous contrast in style. They responded:

Journalist 1: It is an interesting pattern, and I would probably agree with you that that is the way it works to a certain extent. Now, I would caution you that *RT* is a state media, and make sure you emphasize the difference [between state and private media,] because I have never myself nor none of my journalist friends that I am aware of have ever been instructed to cover a story a certain way or even felt pressured to cover a story a certain way because, while we may have opinion sides of our publications which are heavily politically bent one way or the other, it does not really trickle down in my experience to a news floor. So I have never been told by an editor or definitely some other person how to cover it. I would say that you are on to something but I would not venture as far to say that in US publications everyone is a much better journalist or much more impartial or something like that, but certainly when I see *RT's* coverage, I get the sense that it is guided by a political objective.

The journalist understood the question to be "why is *RT* so biased and yours so good?" They conclude that the reason *RT's* coverage is different to the West's is that *RT* is state-owned and politically motivated, unlike Western media. The idea that the Western media may be biased was not even considered. One idea that sprang to mind was that journalists for American and British organizations were simply better and more impartial. The coverage that presented Venezuela favourably was "guided by a political objective" while the coverage that, as noted above, portrays Venezuela in a negative light is objective and balanced. Some journalists are so immersed in ideology that they do not even recognize they are underwater.

The same journalist was asked whether big businesses could be swaying the coverage or whether political biases could be intruding. Clearly skeptical of this but trying to be convivial, they responded:

Journalist 1: Yeah, sure, it could be, I guess. As somebody who is involved in making the sausage, I will be honest with you: I don't know where that would come from. So if

> you were to do a revision of my stories, I would say
> probably more often than not they do not paint a very
> glowing picture of what is happening here. But that is
> just what I see happening.

The journalist agreed that Western coverage was negative and that Russian coverage was positive but explicitly denied that there was an imposed editorial line or government or corporate interference. So there must be another explanation. Journalists are clearly aware of alternative explanations of events, but they dismiss them as illogical or politically motivated. Essentially, the reason offered for remarkable similarity of reporting is that this is the objective reality, or close to it. This journalist was "right-thinking". But as cataloged in Chapters 1–5, this is not a cohesive argument whatsoever.

When pushed it is clear that most journalists wholeheartedly buy into the official narrative. Unlike Philo and Berry's (2004, 2011) studies of the media's pro-Israel coverage of the Israel-Palestine conflict, which found that many journalists were sympathetic to the Palestinians but felt under a great deal of pressure from their editors and from flak from Israeli government sources, most journalists covering Venezuela were not at all sympathetic to the *chavistas*. Their similar stance to the US government is a reflection of the power of the hegemonic narrative that dominates the public sphere on Venezuela. Journalists were aware that inside of the country the government and significant portions of the population had opposing views on major issues and treated them with mistrust. However, they considered these views to be illogical, at best. We saw this in the reporting as well. For example, *The Daily Telegraph* (2002) treated the idea of US involvement in the 2002 coup, since proven correct, as absurd, noting, "the last thing the Americans need is a new set of myths about Yanqui coup-mongering". The question could certainly be asked whether journalists invested in a controversial topic such as Venezuela would admit their misgivings to a researcher. However, it appeared that some, if not most, of the journalists did not even consider their work controversial, having never come across serious criticism of it.

Justin Delacour argued that the absence of journalists who take an opposing stance to their governments' positions is proof of "pressure to toe a certain line". No doubt there is some truth to this. If a journalist begins to constantly challenge the government line, it is unlikely they will be rehired, let alone promoted. Bart Jones confirmed he sometimes moderated what he wrote to toe a line while Matt Kennard admitted that he did not even bother to submit ideas contrary to the editorial line of his newspaper. But those who consistently produce content critical of the Venezuelan government have not faced significant problems because their opinions largely coincide with those of their editors, owners, advertisers and their government. Thus, they are correct in stating that they are free to write how they want, because what they want to write pleases their superiors. They are indeed free to say what they want. But if they had alternative opinions, they would not be where they are.

Journalists have been preselected from a pool of privileged candidates who share largely the same worldview as the government and the owners of major media. On the topic of Venezuela, they often arrive largely ignorant about the country but with preconceptions already shaped by the media. Those interviewed are far more knowledgeable about the country than those stationed in London or New York who are instructed to piece together a story. Journalists who write stories about Venezuela are often foreign affairs correspondents or simply staff journalists, writing about Vladimir Putin on Monday, television programmes on Tuesday, and about Nicolas Maduro on Wednesday. These time-starved employees do not have time to do background reading to construct an opposing narrative and likely read only the last three or four reports their newspaper did on the country. In that sense, the coverage is self-perpetuating. As Julia Buxton said, "I think a lot of journalists just do not have the intellectual framework to understand what is going on in Venezuela." They would be sticking their head above the parapet writing something that contradicts the hegemonic framing of the country. If they wished to do so they would need a rock-solid intellectual framework and to be sure of the facts and figures. It would take a considerable amount of reading to be confident in taking a stand. Making mistakes while countering the dominant narrative is a sure fire way to court criticism, mockery, or worse. Making a mistake in an article that regurgitates the prevailing tone is certainly not a career-ending mistake. Journalists simply do not have the time or will to do so. It is simply easier for time-pressed journalists to cut and paste together something from *Reuters* or the last three articles the newspaper ran than to build up something from scratch. Indeed, some might say this is exactly what journalism has become. Journalists who live in Venezuela have the time to build up a detailed knowledge of the country. But, as we have seen in Chapters 6–8, there are other factors that influence how they view the country. Therefore, the hegemonic ideas of the elite stay largely uncontested.

Nevertheless, some journalists, using alternative media and other avenues of knowledge, do build up an alternative understanding. On rare occasions, writers adopt a contrarian position. However, in a sea of negative information their articles seem odd, at best.

From afar it is easy to observe the output of media on Venezuela and see a deterministic, top-down editorial line structure where it is a geopolitical enemy of the US and UK and therefore cynically attacked with deliberately misleading propaganda. However, close contact with the journalists seems to suggest otherwise. While most stories about Venezuela that take longer than an hour or so for a journalist to write must be cleared with an editor or a team of higher-ups in Sao Paulo, New York or London, most journalists insisted that they felt little pressure from editors to toe a line. Why they feel no pressure is not because there is none, but rather because they share a set of assumptions about the government, the role of Western countries in Venezuela, and about the way an economy should be run. For most journalists, there is no noticeable editorial line. Only dissenting journalists feel pressure to produce output contrary to their own views, but there are few of these, because new journalists come from a pre-selected pool of applicants and because of their social surroundings when living in Venezuela. The groupthink created is crucial to understanding the Venezuelan case. If these journalists were left completely to their own devices on what to write, they would write largely the same content as they do currently because their views are in alignment with the newspapers' owners and their governments. Some journalists, such as Kennard and Jones, did build up alternative analyses of the situation thanks to their unconventional backgrounds. Kennard from his theoretical background and Jones because he spent time living in the slums as a lay worker. Yet, the majority of journalists covering Venezuela, coming from similar backgrounds and immersed in a culture antithetical to the Venezuelan government, produce similarly negative content. And that is how the desired outcome of one-sided reporting is achieved. Coercion in the form of editorial control, blacklisting or government interference is used, but is rarely necessary as journalists are willing, committed, sincere volunteers in the media war against Venezuela.

References

Beeton, D., Johnston, J. and Main, A. (2015) "Venezuela," in Wikileaks (ed.) *Wikileaks: The World According to the US Empire*, London: Verso.

Bennett, L. (2001) *News: The Politics of Illusion*, Fourth Edition, London: Longman.

Blum, W. (2003) *Killing Hope: US Military and CIA Interventions Since World War II*, London: Zed Books.

Brouwer, S. (2011) *Revolutionary Doctors: How Venezuela and Cuba Are Changing the World's Conception of Health Care*, New York: Monthly Review Press.

CEPALSTAT (2016a) "Venezuela: National Socio-Demographic Profile," *CEPAL*, http://interwp.cepal.org/cepalstat/Perfil_Nacional_Social.html?pais=VEN&idioma=english

The Daily Telegraph (2002) "Venezuela's Bad Apple," April 13th.

Davies, N. (2009) *Flat Earth News: An Award-winning Reporter Exposes Falsehood, Distortion and Propaganda in the Global Media*, London: Vintage.

Delacour, J. (2005) "The Op-Ed Assassination of Hugo Chavez," *Fair.org*, http://fair.org/extra-online-articles/the-op-ed-assassination-of-hugo-chvez/7/?issue_area_id=9

Gosztola, K. (2017) "Interview With Abby Martin and Michael Prysner on Venezuelan Opposition and Attacks on Journalism," *Shadowproof*, June 11th, https://shadowproof.com/2017/06/11/interview-martin-prysner-venezuelan-opposition-violence/

The Guardian (2007) "Ahmadinejad Seeks to Strengthen South America Ties," September 27th.

Herman, E. and Chomsky, N. (1988) *Manufacturing Consent: The Political Economy of the Mass Media*, New York: Pantheon.

Herman, E. and Chomsky, N. (2002) *Manufacturing Consent: The Political Economy of the Mass Media*, New York: Pantheon.

Lupien, P. (2013) "The Media in Venezuela and Bolivia: Attacking the 'Bad Left' From Below," *Latin American Perspectives*, 40, pp. 226–246.

Miami Herald (2013) "In South Florida, Venezuelans React to Hugo Chavez's Death," March 5th.

NASDAQ (2017) "Crude Oil," www.nasdaq.com/markets/crude-oil.aspx?timeframe=25y

Parenti, M. (1993) *Inverting Reality: The Politics of News Media*, New York: St. Martin's Press.

Philo, G. and Berry, M. (2004) *Bad News From Israel*, London: Pluto.

Philo, G. and Berry, M. (2011) *More Bad News From Israel*, London: Pluto.

Rohter, L. (2010) *Brazil on the Rise: The Story of a Country Transformed*, Basingstoke: Palgrave Macmillan.

Walser, R. (2010) "State Sponsors of Terrorism: Time to Add Venezuela to the List," *The Hertiage Foundation*, January 20th, www.heritage.org/research/reports/2010/01/state-sponsors-of-terrorism-time-to-add-venezuela-to-the-list

Weisbrot, M. (2014) "US Support for Regime Change in Venezuela Is a Mistake," *The Guardian*, February 18th, www.theguardian.com/commentisfree/2014/feb/18/venezuela-protests-us-support-regime-change-mistake

Young, K. (2013) "The Good, the Bad, and the Benevolent Interventionist: U.S. Press and Intellectual Distortions of the Latin American Left," *Latin American Perspectives*, 40:3 (May), pp. 207–225.

Conclusion

Below is a summary of the key findings discussed in the previous chapters.

Key findings

- There was a markedly limited range of opinions offered across the Western press, with differences between newspapers more on style and tone rather than on substance. There was considerable uniformity on how a wide range of newspapers covered one of the most contentious areas in world politics.
- Going against the best empirical evidence available, the Western press overwhelmingly presented Venezuela as a former democracy slipping into dictatorship.
- There was a widespread contempt or even hatred of everything the *chavistas* stood for, expressed in articles, especially editorials.
- Pro-Venezuelan government arguments and sources were largely absent. When included they were often misrepresented or ridiculed.
- "The death of the foreign correspondent": only one full-time correspondent for the English-language Western press in Venezuela.
- Massive cuts to newsroom budgets, leading to reliance on local stringers. Local journalists recruited from highly adversarial Venezuelan opposition-aligned press, leading to a situation where Venezuelan opposition ideas and talking points have their amplitude magnified. Anti-government activists producing supposedly objective news content for Western media.
- Newsroom culture strongly opposed to *chavistas*. Journalists unsympathetic to *chavistas* felt free to write as they wished while journalists with government sympathies had to temper what they wrote and practice self-censorship.

- Experts sympathetic to the *chavistas* "really commonly" black-listed by Western media.

As emphasized throughout this book, events in Venezuela are some of the most widely and hotly contested in modern politics, with an extraordinarily wide range of opinions put forward by governments, NGOs and academia on every issue. However, there was a markedly limited range of opinions offered by Western press, with differences between liberal and conservative, American and British newspapers being more about tone and style, rather than about substance and political stances. Mirroring the stances taken by Western governments, most prominently the American one, every newspaper studied took an aggressive, adversarial position towards the Venezuelan government on a wide range of issues studied. The result was an overwhelmingly negative picture built up of Venezuela's radical political experiment, with articles that put the country in a bad light prevalent, and with positive news stories unpublished. As such, the media effectively only published *bad news* from Venezuela.

In general, the US and conservative press displayed more blistering hostility to the Venezuelan government than the British or liberal press, with the conservative American *Miami Herald* displaying the most outright aversion of everything the *chavistas* stood for. However, the distance between the liberal British *Guardian* and *The Miami Herald* was sufficiently narrow to allow the same journalists to write for both newspapers.

There were far fewer pro-government arguments and sources, with none whatsoever appearing in many articles. When included, they were often misrepresented and ridiculed. For example, in Chapter 5, we saw that much of the press treated the allegation of the *guarimbas* being an attempt to oust the government with US support as a preposterous conspiracy theory. The newspapers in the study consistently repeated the opposition's talking points, such as crime, insecurity and the country being a dictatorship, and ignored the government's, such as improvements in healthcare, education and democracy. There was also an emphasis on the government's wrongdoings and a de-emphasis on the opposition's misdeeds, such as during the 2013 election (see Chapter 4). It was, therefore, the opposition and the US government that set the agenda for what was and was not newsworthy in the media.

The press also consistently presented allegations as facts and facts as mere allegations when it suited their position. They presented arguments by critics of the Venezuelan government and opposition talking points as facts and the opposite side of the argument, if at all, as ludicrous and risible, believed only by conspiracy theorists. In Chapter 4 were saw how most newspapers repeated the highly dubious opposition *allegation* that Chavez personally ordered snipers to mow down his own supporters during the 2002 coup as an established, uncontested *fact* which therefore "justified" (*The Times*, 2002) every criticism of him, and, presumably, his overthrow. Meanwhile, the *fact* of US involvement was presented merely as an *allegation*: a weak allegation made by officials the newspapers had spent years demonizing and immediately countered.

The opposing side of the debate was very often marginalized or absent altogether. Highly contested opposition arguments were presented largely as uncontroversial facts, giving the reader the impression there was no debate whatsoever. This is a problem in itself. Yet it is made worse when looking at the basic empirical data from well-known and respected polls, surveys and statistics from highly credible sources such as the United Nations and World Bank, which very often suggested a completely different conclusion to that the media presented. For example, in Chapter 3, we saw how the media claimed social indicators had fallen under Chavez, in complete contrast to the empirical data. The media are well aware of the data, as they often cherry-picked parts of the surveys to present a different picture of the country. Thus, the press can be said to have produced *bad news* from Venezuela in another sense: fake news, biased, without balance and an absence of a facts-based approach.

The second part of the thesis attempted to explain the question of why the country was covered in this way; what factors influenced its output.

Crucial in understanding the reporting is the geopolitical context underpinning it. After Hugo Chavez was elected, the government managed to revive the OPEC cartel and radically raise oil prices, meaning the US and much of Europe were paying hundreds of billions of dollars extra for oil. Venezuela was also at the epicentre of a Latin American challenge to Western imperialism in Latin America, with a new wave of left-of-centre Latin American governments openly challenging Western (particularly US) power and profit. New leaders like Lula in Brazil, Morales in Bolivia, Correa in Ecuador and Fernandez in Argentina came to power openly challenging American dominance. However, Chavez was unquestionably the chief architect of the "pink tide", and created new international organizations designed at advancing Latin America unity to the detriment of the US. As such, it represented the strongest challenge to American dominance since the Cuban Revolution of 1959.

However, there were more explanatory factors that created this perfect storm of bad news. Chapter 6 discussed how journalists increasingly come from privileged backgrounds, attending elite universities and live in rich metropolises, leading to a narrowing of opinions and outlooks expressed in print. As the interviewees confided, journalists sent to Venezuela are parachuted in without expertise or great understanding of the country, and often without the ability to speak Spanish – in other words to communicate properly with the bottom 90–95 percent of the population. Journalists are overwhelmingly housed in the wealthy Chacao district of Eastern Caracas. This is important as Caracas, like many cities in the developing world, is highly segregated along class lines, with millions of poor, darker-skinned Venezuelans living in *barrios*, shantytowns on the hills surrounding the city, while much of Eastern Caracas is a walled off island of luxury. Class is the fundamental fault line along which the highly polarized Venezuelan society is split, with lower-class Venezuelans strongly supporting the government and the higher-classes strongly opposing it. As the ability to speak English is correlated with socioeconomic status around the developing world, journalists who cannot speak Spanish tend to stay in Chacao, as they can only be confident of being able to speak to locals in the municipality. This, combined with concerns over crime creates a situation where journalists inordinately spend their work and leisure time in an opposition bastion. Hence, it can appear to a journalist that "everyone" has a negative opinion about the government. This is because they are meeting a pre-selected subset of the population that coincides closely with opposition supporters.

We are living through a sustained and possibly terminal collapse in newspaper sales. Coupled with that is the reduction in advertising revenues received due to increased online competition. Consequently, newspapers have furiously cut staffing costs, downsizing their total staff and their budget. This has led to the death of the foreign correspondent; this study found that there is only one full-time correspondent in Venezuela for all Western English-language newspapers. Work has instead been outsourced to freelancers, local journalists and news agencies like *Reuters* and *Bloomberg*. However, they are under the same financial squeeze as the newspapers. They also employ cheaper, local Venezuelan journalists as opposed to flying Westerners out.

These journalists largely come from elite backgrounds working in established local news organizations in Caracas. As discussed in Chapter 7, these organizations were usually radically anti-*chavista* and strongly aligned with the opposition and took a lead role in attempts to depose the government. Therefore, Venezuelan journalists tend to hold strongly anti-government views. While providing valuable local expertise, the presence of local journalists led to a newsroom atmosphere that was *highly* adversarial to the government. The local media orchestrated and supported numerous attempts at regime change, like the coup covered in Chapter 2, where many participated in the arrests and torture of political and media opponents.

Dissenting journalists revealed that this led to a newsroom full of people who considered themselves activists, the "resistance" and the "dissidents" at war with a tyrannical government, and felt it was their duty to "get rid of Chavez" by any means necessary. Truth is always the first casualty in war, and some journalists writing for the Western press are effectively anti-government activists. Their role as journalists for major Venezuelan newspapers gave them credibility in the eyes of international news organizations and led to a situation where the opposition's narrative was repeated and amplified across the world. However, this is not purely by accident. There are a good number of Venezuelan journalists sympathetic to the government. Any of them could have been hired to work for international organizations as well. But this has not happened. The effect of this is that "unbiased", "objective" Western news is not dissimilar to opposition propaganda.

There is, therefore, a discreet but coercive and overwhelming cultural dynamic at play. Western journalists arriving without knowledge of the country are immersed into this culture. The opposition, made up substantially of English-speaking, light-skinned, well-spoken professionals are careful to cultivate good relations with foreign journalists. Journalists are often shown round by fixers, polite, well-spoken locals who insist the dictatorial government is destroying the country. This computes with their preconceptions of the place. Why would they question it? In contrast, the dark-skinned poor *chavistas*, with whom they share little in common and do not interact with on a day-to-day basis, treat them with suspicion or outright hostility, seeing them as propagandists trying to overthrow their democracy. Consequently, journalists unsurprisingly fall into the anti-government world, with those who do reporting they feel very little or no pressure to toe a certain line. Going against the dominant view that the *chavistas* represent anything other than a "Nazi blitzkrieg", as one interviewee said, will bring strife, arguments, or worse, as seen in Chapter 6.

There are also structural constraints that all journalists agreed affected their work. For more substantial pieces requiring more resources, journalists must have their pitch approved by bosses who are often in London or New York, and these bosses sometimes send down ideas for stories for them. Therefore, bosses on different continents with limited knowledge about the country are shaping what becomes news in Venezuela. Journalists are also under severe time pressure to produce increasingly larger amounts of content for print and online publication, leading to a lack of depth to many stories. This lack of depth is exacerbated by tight word limits imposed, meaning there is no time or space for in-depth coverage or to challenge running narratives. Furthermore, the need to generate interest and draw an audience leads to the press running inflammatory or exaggerated stories, in other words, by publishing *bad* or fake news.

However, much of the news on Venezuela is not even written by those living there. Western journalists with little knowledge of the country are often parachuted into Caracas for a day or two, where they meet English-speaking sources in exclusive parts of the city and then leave. The idea they could report accurately is certainly questionable, but they are at least near the action. Yet, due to cost-cutting measures, much of the coverage of Venezuela is not even written from the country, rather by Latin America correspondents in Rio or Bogota or even by ordinary, highly time-pressed journalists in the UK or US. The result is a lack of originality and conformity with the dominant narrative, as these journalists do not have the time or background knowledge to challenge it.

This book started by laying out two theoretical frameworks of understanding media coverage. Parenti's (1993: 186) four rules of how the media cover left-wing Latin American nations predict that there would be an absence of any positive coverage of democratic and economic reform, a portrayal of the rich elites as suffering oppression, silence on the nefarious actions of the US government and a presentation of the economy in disarray due to socialism's inherent flaws.

We saw the first rule throughout the study, notably in Chapter 1, which presented the democratic reforms supported and approved of by the large majority as leading the country towards dictatorship. In Chapters 2 and 5, we saw that the media presented those attempting to overthrow the government violently as peaceful democratic activists oppressed by a brutal regime, while in Chapters 2 and 5, we saw how the US role in the 2002 coup and the 2014 *guarimbas* was rarely brought up, except to dismiss it as an example of the nonsensical paranoia of the *chavistas*. This held largely true for even the British newspapers. Finally, we saw in Chapter 5, how the reason given for the protests was the government's economic incompetence, and not that it was a well-designed coup attempt backed by the US government. As one op-ed put it, the country was "a political and economic tragedy of catastrophic proportions" because of "failed policies based on Marxist ideology and class hatred" (*Miami Herald*, 2013).

Herman and Chomsky (2002) argued that news is presented in a way conducive to elite interests through a series of five filters: elite ownership of the media, reliance on advertising from big business, reliance on official sources, flak and anti-socialist bias. Their Propaganda Model predicts overly negative coverage of the country due to the geopolitical reasons explored in the introduction and Chapter 8.

Many of the filters were brought up by the interviewees; indeed, many explicitly referenced the model. Elite ownership and advertising influenced the output of the news. Sourcing was doubly important to Venezuela, as Western government officials continually shaped the news by releasing highly combative and negative statements about the country (for example, Ed Royce's statement in Chapter 3). The Venezuelan elite, comprising of pollsters, journalists, church and union leadership and big business owners among others, are highly antagonistic and openly insurrectionary in their outlook, and these figures' comments also were a factor. Journalists and academics, both ones that wrote positively about Venezuela, like Dan Beeton, and negatively, like Jim Wyss, confirmed they received flak for not being sufficiently hard on the government (see Chapter 8). The anti-socialist bias of the media was evident throughout the sample. For example, in Chapter 3, we saw that the media presented Hugo Chavez's legacy as one of "decay and dysfunction" brought on by a "bungling" Chavez, who destroyed the economy and the country's once democratic institutions and the free-market trying to "impose pseudo-Marxism".

However, there were more factors than these that influenced the reporting of the country. Coercion in the newsroom does exist: Matt Kennard confirmed phrases and sentences that did not fit the established narrative were removed by editors and Bart Jones felt he sometimes had to temper what he was writing. Furthermore, academics who held sympathetic views to the *chavistas* were "really commonly" blacklisted from the media, and not just from an individual newspaper. However, most journalists interviewed claimed they felt no significant pressure and did not know of any colleague who said they did. Not coincidentally, all these journalists reproduced the conventional narrative on Venezuela. They are right to say they do not feel pressure, not because there is none, but because they share the dominant, hegemonic, neoliberal worldview of owners and advertisers.

Herman and Chomsky explained the creation of the environment through the pre-selection of "right-thinking personnel" by the staff and management's internalization of and adaptation to the values and priorities of ownership, advertisers and government power (2002: preface). This study is therefore in complete agreement with the authors, finding most journalists *felt* free to write what they want about Venezuela. However, if they believed something different, they would not be where they are today. The result is *bad news*.

Although this book is ostensibly about Venezuela, it actually tells us more about the structure of Western media and how it functions. Our media is severely hindered by the structural and cultural factors highlighted throughout this book. This is incredibly important as the media have a profound power in reflecting and constructing the world that the public is exposed to, to manipulate and control what we understand to be possible. It is the authority for what is true and what is false, what is possible and what is impossible. There is perhaps no greater power in today's society. That is why it is crucial to understand and critique how they function. How the media treat alternative models of society like Venezuela is key in influencing how the public understand their own society and alternatives to the *status quo*. It follows that holding them to account is equally crucial.

References

Chomsky, N. (1989) *Necessary Illusions: Thought Control in Democratic Societies*, London: Pluto Press.

Herman, E. and Chomsky, N. (2002) *Manufacturing Consent: The Political Economy of the Mass Media*, New York: Pantheon.

Miami Herald (2013) "Venezuela's Hugo Chavez and His US Business Partners," March 2nd.

Parenti, M. (1993) *Inverting Reality: The Politics of News Media*, New York: St. Martin's Press.

The Times (2002) "No Bolivar," April 13th.

Index

Page numbers in **bold** indicate tables on the corresponding pages.

Printed in the United States
by Baker & Taylor Publisher Services